Further education in the market place

The post-sixteen sector of education has been subjected to a considerable degree of change in the wake of the 1992 Further and Higher Education Act. The pressures of incorporation have tended to concentrate attention on organisation and management structures, and strategic and business planning. There is now a real need to reconsider the functions, priorities and values of further education.

This book is designed for college staff, and in particular members of college boards. It explores some of the major issues involved in college development and focuses on specific areas which must be tackled if colleges are to meet the education and training needs of the majority of young people and adults.

Jean McGinty, a former HMI, has a national knowledge of further education, works as a consultant and is a governor of a number of colleges. **John Fish** was an HMI adviser to the Warnock Committee, has acted as a consultant to UNESCO, OECD/CERI, and ILEA and is a college governor.

Further education in the market place

Equity, opportunity and individual learning

Jean McGinty and John Fish

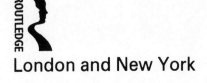

London and New York

First published 1993
by Routledge
11 New Fetter Lane, London EC4P 4EE

Simultaneously published in the USA and Canada
by Routledge
29 West 35th Street, New York, NY 10001

Typeset in Palatino by
NWL Editorial Services, Langport, Somerset

Printed and bound in Great Britain by
Mackays of Chatham PLC, Chatham, Kent

British Library Cataloguing in Publication Data
A catalogue record for this book is available from the
British Library

Library of Congress Cataloging in Publication Data
McGinty, Jean, 1928 –
  Further education in the market-place: equity, opportunity,
  and individual learning/ Jean McGinty and John Fish.
    p. cm.
  Includes bibliographical references and index.
  ISBN 0–415–10040–2. — ISBN 0–415–10041–0 (pbk.)
    1. Education, Higher—Great Britain—Aims and objectives.
2. Universities and colleges—Great Britain—Administration.
I. Fish, John. II. Title.
LA637.M36 1993
378.41–dc20   93–7346
                                                            CIP

ISBN 0–415–10040–2   ISBN 0–415–10041–0 (pbk)

Contents

List of figures   vi
Preface   vii
Acknowledgements   x

Part I The background to change

1 Vision, values and vulnerability   3

2 The recent history of further education   16

3 Recent influences   28

4 Potential students   38

5 The college response – the elements   49

6 The college response – current structures   62

Part II Developing further education

7 The parameters   75

8 A college agenda   92

9 Implications for college governors and managers   102

10 A way ahead   113

Bibliography   122
Index   126

Figures

5.1 The traditional curriculum model   58

5.2 The learner-led model   58

7.1 Developing a rationale   91

9.1 Core elements   105

9.2 Common necessary elements   105

9.3 Specific necessary elements   106

9.4 The FEFC Strategic Planning Framework   112

Preface

This book has been written in the midst of a major upheaval in the further education system. For this reason what is presented here is a snapshot in time. As new procedures are being implemented conclusions can only be tentative. In the recent past colleges have been preoccupied with the nuts and bolts of incorporation. Organisation and management structures and strategy and business plans have drawn attention away from educational aspects of college work. The period following incorporation may be a valuable time to reconsider the purposes and values of further education.

One objective of writing this book is to inform members of college boards, now responsible for colleges of further education, about the recent history of colleges and about some of the major issues concerning their development. The study identifies issues which need to be tackled by colleges if they are to meet the further education and training needs of the majority of young people and adults. While it is assumed that most senior managers in colleges will be familiar with the material in this book, it is also assumed that there are many members of staff of colleges who might appreciate an overview of the contexts in which they work. Similarly, local authority and local education authority administrators may find the book useful. Finally, the authors have kept in mind the informed adult who is increasingly expected to make responsible decisions about educational matters.

The importance of having a vision of the future is stressed, as is the value of an overview as each institution competes for students in a post-school market. The board and senior managers will be entirely responsible for the values the college promotes and for the quality of its facilities, programmes and work.

It is not enough to be businesslike. Sensitivity to community needs, sympathy for the educational and training needs of reluctant learners and a concern for standards in lower-level and less prestigious work are equally important. The inclusive college concerned with all educational needs is seen as a model to aim for. Such a college is accessible and responsive to individual differences. Such aims are not seen as incompatible with efficiency and cost-effectiveness, particularly when the long-term social costs of a poorly trained and unmotivated work-force is recognised.

There is a great deal of material about particular aspects of further education, as the Bibliography indicates, but there appears to be little accessible literature about the field as a whole. The college of further education is a dynamic organisation which needs to be looked at in its entirety. If this book stimulates discussion of its functions, its priorities and above all its values, it will make a useful contribution to a sense of direction for the developing college.

Acknowledgements

Our thanks to the Further Education Unit for use of figures on pp. 106–7 and to the Further Education Funding Council for the use of their figure on p. 133.

Part I

The background to change

Chapter 1

Vision, values and vulnerability

A highly skilled and flexible work-force is an essential element in effective industrial and commercial competition and in successful involvement in a single European market. Comparisons with other countries like Germany and Japan reveal major weaknesses in the standards of education and vocational preparation of many young people and adults in the United Kingdom.

This book is about the contribution that colleges of further education are being asked to make to remedy those weaknesses in a competitive post-sixteen education and vocational training market. It is about the context in which those colleges are responding to change and planning for the future. Colleges are now corporations governed by non-elected boards of volunteers, mainly from business and industry.

It is also about the young people and adults for whom further education and vocational training are vital if they are to have the skills and competences that the labour market needs. These should also include the personal and social competences necessary for becoming contributing citizens in a complex society.

A LONG-STANDING PROBLEM

The hierarchical and academic value system in British education has traditionally accorded scant attention and a low priority to technical education and vocational preparation. The academic education of able and successful young people has been subsidised until they reach their twenties, but until recently further and continuing education was the Cinderella of the system, neglected and undervalued by politicians with little contact with and experience of non-advanced further education.

There has been little public or political support for longer education for limited achievers. Early school-leaving and entry to unskilled work without vocational training was, until relatively recently, the expectation for up to 40 per cent of the school population. It was the high cost of increasing youth unemployment that triggered action, rather than a positive belief in the value of further and vocational education. Even then training, rather than education, was seen as the answer, with untried training agencies often preferred to proven colleges of further education.

In spite of new legislation little change has taken place in an educational value system, based on elitism, where levels of learning are considered of higher value than levels of competence. A funding system which favours the easy to educate and train still takes little account of the expense of inadequately preparing the less motivated and harder to educate for the labour market.

A RENEWED INTEREST

It is now being recognised that our successful partners in Europe have not only always valued extended education for all but have also given equal status to academic and technical skills (FEU 1991a). Attempts are now being made to rectify past neglect and promote effective further education and vocational preparation.

A further stimulus to a renewed interest has been the continuing introduction of new technologies. These have had two major effects on employment:

- the elimination of low-level and unskilled jobs in industry and commerce;
- the introduction of self-service in retail trading.

Education and training programmes have to take these trends into account (FEU 1991b). The introduction of complex technology and machinery demands high levels of functional efficiency. Effective management cannot be maintained without the support of a well-educated work-force and highly skilled technicians. In the United Kingdom value of technical proficiency needs to be recognised and given status by making resources available for the education and training necessary to develop such proficiency.

THE TRADITION

Further and continuing education has traditionally been seen as a way forward by many young people and adults unable to enter higher education and the traditional professions (FEU/REPLAN 1988). It has provided first and second chances not only to acquire technical qualifications but also to achieve academic success and improve general education. From its early night-school days it has supported individual self-improvement.

Colleges traditionally recruited their students from well-motivated individuals seeking educational and technical qualifications and from apprentices sponsored by industry. From the beginning highly motivated adults have been attracted by what colleges have to offer. Now many women are brushing up and developing new skills in order to return to work. Other adults are seeking to upgrade skills and improve their qualifications in the labour market.

More recently further education and training has been seen as one element in the government's concern to improve the skills of an unemployed work-force. Students with more limited educational achievements, often unsuccessful and less motivated learners, have been recruited on a variety of youth training schemes in colleges paid for by government agencies and employers.

THE FUTURE

The government has reorganised the management and financing of further and higher education. Although the process is incomplete at the time of writing, local education authorities (LEAs) are no longer responsible for vocational further education.

Colleges are now independent businesses financed:

- by the Further Education Funding Council (FEFC);
- by Training and Enterprise Councils (TECs) if approved as Training Organisations;
- from a range of other sources prepared to pay for what they have to offer.

The student market is being made more competitive. Schools are being encouraged to provide post-sixteen technical and vocational options. Government policy appears to be to break up a relatively coherent system into competing individual units. Colleges, if they are to survive, will have to offer attractive programmes, designed to meet the needs of training sponsors and students, at competitive costs. It is therefore vital that governors and managers have a sensitive understanding of the place and purpose of the further education college in the education system and in the local community.

Governors must have a vision of the future and a conceptual framework in order successfully to steer their colleges through the jungle of competing pressures and claims (McNay 1991). Similarly, potential sponsors and students need to understand the college system and what further and continuing education can offer them.

THE VISION

The underlying philosophy of further and continuing education, on which this book is based, is that all young people and adults are entitled to educational opportunities which support their career development and enhance their professional and personal knowledge and competence. As part of this aim all young people should have access to full-time post-sixteen education for at least three years at some appropriate time in their lives.

An individual entitlement to further and continuing education should not be wholly dependent on commercial sponsorship or narrowly conceived training. Nor should it be confined solely to the production of marketable skills. It should always include the opportunity for personal development.

While there are good grounds for ensuring that public services, commerce and industry finance some further education and training, the dangers of sponsorship must be recognised. Where programmes develop specific skills which enhance the economic effectiveness of services, industries and businesses, these should be expected to make a contribution.

There are no longer marked differences between the aims of universities, including those that were previously polytechnics, and other contributors to post-school education. The aims of further and higher education should be to increase participation, to achieve higher standards and to make more effective use of available resources (DES 1991).

Although there are different visions of the way ahead which influence priorities and funding, it is hoped that colleges will continue to support an educated competence and recognise it as a more valuable outcome than narrow skill-training. At present some of the funding of non-advanced further education would seem to suggest that a skilled work-force is more important than an educated one.

CHANGE

Educational institutions have been subject to constant change since the beginning of the 1980s (Hall 1990). Despite the continuity of more than twelve years of Conservative government, the long-term development of further education and training has been inhibited by short-term political policies and legislative changes. Changing priorities, new schemes and varying conditions for annual grants have all created uncertainty.

This lack of a consistent and coherent approach has led to staff insecurity and management uncertainty. It has created confusion and tension between aspirations and reality, staff who cope with change and staff who defend against it, staff with vision and staff preoccupied with very short-term problems. These tensions have, in their turn, created uncertainty for students.

Incompatibility between long-term developmental objectives and short-term fashionable objectives is often at the root of much of the current confusion in the post-sixteen world. Responsiveness and change are necessary consequences of a market in further education, but colleges need security and support if they are to develop their contribution.

EDUCATION AND TRAINING

A complex society demands educated as well as trained citizens (CBI 1991). Education for responsible citizenship, although equally important to the effective use of resources, tends to have a lower priority than vocational preparation. The vocational/non-vocational distinctions made in government policies reflect this priority, although both are an integral part of preparation for an active working life and responsible citizenship.

In a complex and competitive labour market, with constantly changing patterns of employment, it is increasingly necessary to recognise a distinction between:

- skills, based on training and the formation of good habits, which can be exercised automatically under stress; and

- competences, based on education, which require the ability to choose, change and make sound judgements.

It may be helpful to look at some differences between skills and competences. The way to acquire a mastery of basic *skills* and good work habits is to undergo well-planned training, a process in which the learner is a relatively passive recipient of instruction. Outcomes and competences are in the form of automatic responses to standard situations. Basic military training is an example of skill-development. Such training ensures that skills are over-learned and habituated so they can be implemented without mistakes under extreme pressure. The exercise of such skills may become automatic in defined circumstances. Similarly, some aspects of education, such as legible writing, good spelling and mental arithmetic, require the training of skills and the development of good habits.

Competences require the development of understanding and a willingness to experiment, to make judgements and to solve problems. Educated competence results in an informed frame of reference being brought to bear imaginatively on a task with the aim of arriving at an appropriate outcome. Such competences, which may be susceptible to pressure and change, are abilities increasingly sought by employers. The way to acquire *competences* which involve knowledge, understanding and judgement is to be educated, a process in which the learner is an active participant. This involves participation, planning learning and the form it might take and negotiating its outcomes. The learner is expected to make a creative contribution to the learning process.

Educated responses to problems and situations should involve imagination and flexibility. The vision of a world-class professional work-force demands an education system from which all young people, whatever their ability or achievements, emerge with well-trained basic skills, appropriate education and positive attitudes to further active learning.

Post-sixteen education and vocational training opportunities need to build on the outcomes of compulsory education and to provide an appropriate balance of skills and understanding, knowledge and judgement; that is to say, a balance of training and education. Both skills and competences, as defined, are necessary in modern industry and commerce. There is no simple equivalence between colleges and training agencies. They are not alternatives nor should they be rivals for funding if an *educated and trained* work-force is the objective.

COLLEGES AND TRAINING AGENCIES

The relationship between education and training implies differences between a college providing education and an agency providing training. But these are far from clear and, like those between vocational and non-vocational education, they may be blurred. They should, nevertheless, be recognised. The CBI report, *Towards a Skills Revolution*, values a broad programme including both education and training.

Differences between colleges and training agencies involve values. A college should offer more choice and a much more comprehensive approach to personal development. Colleges should:

- offer counselling and guidance;
- provide a wide range of options from which individuals may choose;
- have programmes which develop broad general skills transferable from one situation to another;
- be concerned with the personal development of students as well as their progress as learners;
- be interested in the process and quality of learning as well as its outcomes;
- set education and training in a context and ensure that as far as possible its contribution builds on what has gone before and provides an appropriate preparation for what follows.

Training agencies, on the other hand, may be characterised by:

- responsibility for discrete skills and competences;
- concern for outcomes rather than processes;
- the development of discrete skills within a defined time-scale;
- little responsibility for continuity in personal development or learning.

Independence and Values

The Education Reform Act (1988), which also initiated changes in post-sixteen education, required LEAs to produce a strategic plan for further education in their areas. Each college was to produce a development plan to implement the LEA plan. Independence now requires that college plans take account of FEFC priorities as well as those of other funding agencies.

At the heart of the changes in further education, now being put into effect, are profound questions of definition and value. Colleges, with other trainers and TECs, now define the ethics of further education and are responsible for the values of post-school education. Although further education institutions have implicit and explicit values, often differently perceived by learners and teachers, one of the dangers of the commercial approach is that students may be seen as unit costs and products rather than as developing individuals.

Pressures from commerce, industry and the local community, as well as those from a variety of other groups, can only be dealt with within a clear policy framework. As part of this framework, governors and senior managers of colleges need to consider a number of questions:

- What is the purpose of the college?
- Who are its customers?
- What value system and conceptual framework inform college policies and practices?
- Are these values clearly demonstrated in college priorities, policies and practices?

(Commercial development has brought a number of new terms into use in colleges. For example, 'customer' can be used both to refer to *students* receiving education and to *sponsors* of a student's education. The word 'client' may be used, for example in 'client services', to refer to arrangements with *sponsors* of training such as TECs and also to describe support services for *students*. For consistency the word 'student' will be used to refer to all young people and adults undergoing education and training and the word 'sponsor' to refer to all those who pay for education and training.)

The answers to these questions developed in individual colleges will demonstrate the priorities and values of the governors and staff. Quality-assurance procedures instituted by the college should also monitor these values and priorities in practice and ensure that standards are maintained (FEU 1991c; Banks 1992).

In addition to responsibility for a clear policy framework,

governors and senior management teams will be expected to administer colleges on sound commercial lines with the objectives of efficiency, growth and profit. But businesses do not always prosper, and in a competitive system colleges may expect to become involved in take-overs, mergers and indeed in bankruptcy. (FEFC 1992b).

Values and equity

Few would quarrel with the idea of value for money in terms of the standards of what you buy. A course or training module should be considered in terms of value for money. However, real dangers arise when value for money is associated with the value of those being educated or trained. Equity is threatened if student groups become characterised in terms of whether they are worth training or not.

It is important to distinguish between equality and equity. Giving the same opportunities to everyone may be a form of equality, as would entering everybody, regardless of age and condition, in the same race. Equity demands a more subtle approach where opportunities which are different are resourced adequately and given the same status. The concept of equity demands that the system of financing education and training does not discriminate unfairly between 'high-value' and 'low-value' students.

While it is very easy to appreciate the value added to the economy by 'high-value' groups, the social cost of not providing education and training for groups with apparent 'low value', in terms of unemployment benefits and social security payments, may go unrecognised. These considerable costs do not fall on non-inclusive and inappropriate further and continuing education but are nevertheless met by public monies. Education is rewarded for success but seldom penalised for failure.

Inequalities resulting from different levels of financial support for schools, often based on the perceived academic value of their pupils, are all too apparent. Further education has had the reputation of redressing this imbalance. Short-term 'value-for-money' decisions related to student groups may perpetuate the worst features of the school system without raising general standards.

Values and colleges

The history of further education colleges has been one of responding to educational and vocational training needs. Their work is based on a number of assumptions about the educational process which are currently being challenged. The more independent colleges become, the greater the necessity for them to be clear about their purpose in a field where there are many other training agencies.

(Executive agencies have been set up by the government to manage certain functions. For example, in the field of employment the 'Training Agency' was set up to promote, finance and evaluate youth and employment training. Now other 'agencies' are funded by TECs to deliver specified training contracts, as are colleges when they are approved training organisations. Throughout this book 'agency' will be used to describe independent non-government organisations in the post-sixteen market.)

A number of questions, to which there are no easy answers, are raised when colleges become competing units in a further education and training market. These questions include:

- Is a college simply an administrative convenience for the delivery of courses and training programmes?
- Is it an economic way to deliver the education and training modules common to a wide range of education and training needs?
- Is it important that the college provides opportunities for social interaction and shared learning?
- Is its primary purpose to respond to needs identified by local and regional industry or to broader national needs?

The educational tradition is that the college has wider responsibilities for its students than a training agency. It should give consideration to community needs as well as those of commerce and industry and it should promote personal development as well as the acquisition of employment-related competences. These well-tried educational objectives may be less easy to achieve in a competitive market.

Vulnerability

There has never been any period in the development of further education when well- motivated young people and adults have not taken advantage of what it offers. But certain groups have always found difficulty in gaining access to further education, and are vulnerable to market forces. Their needs may be different, difficult to meet and costly, generating insufficient income or profit.

Minority interests are not always well served by business and commerce. In recent years further education has made real attempts to meet minority education and training needs and it is to be hoped that a more businesslike approach will not reduce opportunities for such groups.

Accountability and value for money have been important aspects of recent policies. Resource limitations have resulted in the worthwhileness of the education and training of individuals being a factor in provision. The vision of further education and the values it may be forced to accept may result in some college work with minority groups becoming vulnerable.

Colleges may be unable to provide training programmes and modules which are expensive and staff-intensive unless their full costs are met by a sponsor. Less obvious further educational needs in the community may receive lower priority than more prestigious but ephemeral commercial and media fashions for which there are funds.

If minority interests are not strongly defended by colleges, and funding agencies will not finance such education and training, individuals may become handicapped by a lack of access to preparation for employment. By 1991, after just one year's experience, TECs, for example, were pleading that their financial situation made it difficult for them to pay for training for disabled people and that this cost should be borne by central government.

The 'value-added' concept of educational outcomes may also result in more limited opportunities for those with learning difficulties or those who need more time than others to reach the same standards. Similarly, small colleges may be vulnerable because they cannot provide for students competitively in terms of education and training costs. There is a real danger that new funding arrangements will encourage colleges to recruit the cheapest to train and that such provision will not reflect community needs.

Governors and senior managers of colleges will be under great pressure to concentrate on those who are easy to educate and train. There will be great temptations to share generated income on the basis of priority for the highest-value groups. Colleges will need to be aware of vulnerable groups in the communities they serve and to provide equal opportunities for them.

The Disenchanted

Schools have not generally served less academic pupils well. Numerous reports have shown how their education has been under-resourced and inappropriate. In city areas many young people are disenchanted with school and reject further and continuing education. Lack of success in school and long-term unemployment combine to produce individuals who support themselves through short-term involvement in paid schemes, course-hopping, benefits and active involvement in a black economy.

Many of those young people live in families where there has been no regular employment for decades. Their living patterns are disorganised and they are disenchanted with the 'system' and reject it. Where individuals rely on external controls, whether these are economic or policing, an expectation that individuals will manage their own lives effectively may be unrealistic. Schemes which motivate most people may not work with them.

These young people and adults present a difficult challenge to post-school education and training services because the current market philosophy of choice and personal responsibility depends on individuals with internalised controls. There are no easy answers to recovering lost generations for whom education and training are areas of failure and rejection, but this problem must be tackled.

The college as a vital centre

Colleges play vital roles in the community they serve. To sustain these roles they must make a balanced response to all the demands made on them. They must be flexible and responsive to new influences and new educational needs. At the same time colleges must be accepting and inclusive in order to meet the widest possible range of student needs (FESC 1989).

The college stands at the intersection of a great many threads in the personal and career development of individuals. It has the potential to provide continuity between different phases of education, personal life and employment. It is also at the interface between many aspects of commercial and community activity.

A period in college may be a vital stage in growing up for a young person leaving school as well as a period of vocational preparation. It may play a vital part in facilitating a woman's return to work and enabling adults at all stages of their lives to upgrade their skills. It may help a member of an ethnic minority to have access to education and training. Equally, a college can collaborate with a wide range of public and private employers to develop appropriate education and training for their employees.

THE FUTURE

The long-term effects of the Further and Higher Education Act (1992) are uncertain. Colleges are developing as separate entrepreneurial businesses under new employer-led boards. Their sources of funding, particularly the FEFC and TECs, are now influencing their priorities. Budget cuts are making change difficult to implement and may be inhibiting provision for less financially rewarding minority needs and interests. However, the value of further education is again being recognised by the government. The sorry record of post-school provision in comparison with European partners is being acknowledged. There is a new hope that a better-educated and prepared work-force can be developed.

New policies are intended to create optimism. The White Paper (DES 1991) states that a major aim is 'to knock down barriers to opportunity. We want higher standards. We want more choice. In short our aim is to give every one of England's young people the chance to make the most of his/her particular talents and to have the best possible start in life.'

It could be argued that current education and training policies are not likely to result in a market. What they are producing is a hierarchy of vocational usefulness to supplement the traditional academic one. A true market economy would be concerned with the whole population, not just with those being educated and trained. It would be concerned with the *costs* of wastage, that is to say, the social security and other financial support provided for individuals as a result of poor education, training and preparation for an effective adult working life.

Chapter 2

The recent history of further education

Change has been a regular feature of post-school provision in further and continuing education. Colleges have always responded to new patterns of employment and student demand. The aspirations of school leavers alter from generation to generation as do the skills and knowledge required for different areas of employment. Qualifications change and young people and adults expect to acquire new competences.

The delivery of further and continuing education has had to be flexible. Full-time and part-time attendance and a pattern of day and night classes used to be the norm. More recently, twilight classes have provided further opportunities, and in some colleges the traditional academic year of forty weeks has been stretched, with facilities used for fifty weeks a year.

Further education in colleges has been supplemented with outreach work providing education and training in business premises, factories, hospitals and other institutions (FEU/REPLAN 1988b). A national system of defined levels of vocational qualification is currently being developed.

It is often the recent past which has the most influence on the way change is accepted and managed. Although there may be more value in looking forward than looking back, the present situation cannot be fully understood without a brief look at recent history.

INDUSTRIAL DEVELOPMENT AND EDUCATION

Colleges of further education have their roots in the desire for new scientific and technical skills stimulated by industrial developments in the early nineteenth century. Evening classes in Mechanics' Institutes were widespread by the second half of the last century. The need for accreditation led first the Royal Society of Arts, and subsequently the City and Guilds of London Institute, to validate courses and examinations. Other regional and professional bodies continued this trend of awarding professional and technical qualifications.

A second thread was the development of technical schools in the early 1900s. These subsequently became part of a tripartite system of secondary, technical and grammar schools in the 1950s. This technical thread disappeared in the compulsory school system with the introduction of comprehensive schools, but its post-sixteen element was continued in further education colleges. Increasing numbers of young people sought academic and technical qualifications as alternatives to programmes delivered in academic sixth forms.

A technical school thread re-emerged in the late 1980s with the setting up of city technical colleges. This was presented as a high-status alternative to local authority schools, which business and industry would be prepared to finance. Its level of funding and high-quality technical facilities were expected to give a new status to technical education.

Onward and upward

Colleges of further education have always been striving for status. The higher the level of academic and technical education, the better it was resourced and the better the staff responsible were paid. Colleges moved from non-advanced to advanced work and established degree courses. Over a period of time some colleges initially became colleges of advanced technology, then poly-technics, and the Further and Higher Education Act (1992) has now enabled them to achieve university status.

This trend has to be recognised. It accounts for the emphasis on higher-level work, the limited priority given to lower-level work and some reluctance to develop programmes suitable for potential students with limited achievements. Franchise arrangements with universities are now reinforcing this reluctance.

DES, LEA, HMI, FESC AND FEU

The immediate post-war period saw an expansion of further education opportunities. The implementation of the 1944

Education Act, the raising of the school-leaving age and increased post-school provision were all part of policies to rebuild Britain after the war and widen the educational opportunities of all children, young people and adults. Local education authorities (LEAs) were responsible for further education which was loosely divided into advanced and non-advanced education.

In some areas considerable civic pride and local industrial interest were evident in the development of colleges. Resources were invested in a range of courses which reflected local industrial and commercial strengths.

LEAs had three main partners in the development of further education:

- Regional Further Education Advisory Councils;
- bodies awarding qualifications (e.g. City and Guilds and similar institutes and professional bodies);
- HM Inspectorate.

Regional Further Education Advisory Councils looked at the pattern of provision in their areas, played a part in determining regional needs, established contacts with other regional planning bodies when these existed and advised LEAs and colleges. LEAs and colleges reviewed established courses and, responding to local and sometimes regional employer needs, made proposals for the development of new ones.

Awarding bodies, in consultation with the other partners, determined:

- the curriculum for specified courses;
- the criteria, standards and examination procedures for qualifications.

HM Inspectorate (HMI) has had a major role in advising the Department of Education and Science (DES) about the quality and appropriateness of the work of colleges. Members of the Inspectorate were associated with a wide variety of professional organisations and examining boards and had a nationwide overview of further education and the needs it was expected to meet. HMI also carried out an inspection programme to inform the DES, LEAs and colleges about the quality and relevance of aspects of further education.

The Inspectorate was in a pivotal position, identifying current LEA and college concerns and passing information about them and the work of colleges upwards to the DES and the government of the day. At the same time HMI was a channel by which government and DES policies and current concerns were transmitted to LEAs and colleges. At that time HMI made recommendations based on regional and national knowledge, and all courses were then authorised by the DES on the recommendation of the HMI regional staff inspector.

The ability of HMI to influence course programmes was gradually eroded and its ability to influence policy has been slowly reduced. Most recent inspections have focused on the ways in which government initiatives are being implemented. Responsibilities for the availability and quality of further education, in all the colleges funded by it, pass in 1993 to the Further Education Funding Council (FEFC), which will make its own inspection arrangements.

Two other organisations have had a major influence on the development of further education, the Further Education Staff College (FESC) and the Further Education Unit (FEU). The FESC, founded in 1960, jointly funded by the DES and LEAs, was envisaged as a centre for policy development, with staff development a major concern from the outset. The College provided a venue where a wide variety of courses and conferences could be based and supported. Emphasis was placed on management education and on increasing the skills of senior college staff. Much recent work has been concerned with the increasing autonomy of colleges and their involvement in resource management and income generation.

The FESC offers consultancy services and is a resource centre offering a range of conference materials. It continues to produce documentation relevant to current issues and to mount a programme of courses delivered at the college and elsewhere.

The FEU, set up more recently, in 1977, has responsibilities for curriculum development in the post-sixteen phase. Since its inception it has been engaged in projects which link Unit staff with the staff of colleges in developing, testing and disseminating curriculum materials. It quickly established a reputation for innovative work with colleges and for practical guidance about the needs of the wider range of students then being recruited to further education.

In April 1992 the Unit for the Development of Adult Continuing Education (UDACE) was incorporated into the FEU. As a result, adequate attention will be given to the development of the Adult

Education Curriculum in close association with further education curriculum development (FEU/UDACE 1992).

INCLUSIVENESS

Until twenty years ago, further education, in association with employer apprenticeship schemes and professional training requirements, could be seen as providing most of the vocational preparation available to young people. It was essentially a selective system providing full-time, part-time, day and block release for courses designed to meet the requirements of a given range of occupations. The content of these courses was based on what professionals, colleges and employers, together with examining bodies, thought should be the skills and knowledge necessary for a given level of operation in industry and commerce.

This time-limited, course-based structure served colleges well, employers perhaps less well, and individual students least well. Individuals took what was on offer, fitting into the available pattern, and sometimes found themselves on inappropriate courses. This approach failed to respond to the continuing educational needs of many adults and low-achieving school leavers and others requiring a less formal structure.

A significant proportion of the school-leaving age group went directly into employment, obtaining jobs that demanded few skills. Colleges offered little below craft level and as a result about 40 per cent of school leavers found no educational and training opportunities after leaving school. The Inner London Education Authority (ILEA) took a lead in supporting provision for this group of young people. In a report, *The Reorganisation of Higher and Further Education*, published in 1975, Appendix II outlined an approach to the needs of school leavers with learning difficulties and limited achievements. It thus became known as Appendix II provision.

The report required every ILEA college to develop work to meet the needs of this group, and at the same time the Authority established a curriculum project to support the work. Other LEAs took similar initiatives but the status of the work remained generally low. With few exceptions lecturers were on the lowest salary scales.

A combination of new technologies and changes in the labour market has reduced the number of jobs for those with limited attainments and vocational skills. High levels of youth unemployment have become common. Vocational training was seen as one means of reducing youth unemployment, and as a result a government-financed employment training agency was set up. The relationship of the agency to further education is discussed below, but the effect of its work was to widen the range of students in colleges.

SCHOOL–COLLEGE LINKS

During the same period school–college links received considerable attention. These links were often haphazard, poorly planned and local. Apart from shared responsibilities for 'O' and 'A' level work there were often marked discontinuities between the school and college sector. Both at national and LEA levels there was no tradition of joint planning.

However, in the 1980s some initiatives were taken. The Technical Vocational Education Initiative (TVEI), started in September 1983, has been influential in forming school–college links. TVEI was conceived as a four-year programme to encourage the development of a vocational proficiency and choice. It formed an element in the curriculum of the last two compulsory school years and a subsequent two years in college.

Although some school–college link courses had existed previously, TVEI became one of the few planned links between school and college. To qualify for funding LEAs had to submit schemes showing how vocational preparation would be enhanced within the school and college curriculum and how the scheme would be implemented and evaluated.

The initiative was intended for pupils of all levels of ability but in practice it has been introduced most widely with less academic pupils. Where TVEI was successful it resulted in a planned four-year programme spanning school and college. A curriculum appropriate for many young people was developed, which included opportunities to experience a number of vocational options. Programmes also provided continuity and progression from school to further education. The introduction of Business Technician Education Certificate (BTEC) courses in schools also stimulated more rigorous and vocationally oriented school–college links.

Improved resources, partnership between the staff of schools and colleges and joint staff development have been fostered. As funding for TVEI is to be progressively withdrawn, it will be interesting to see whether such partnerships will survive in the absence of earmarked funds. Continuity between school and college, however, will remain of considerable importance if colleges are to build effectively on the skills young people acquire before entering them.

FURTHER EDUCATION, THE YOUTH SERVICE AND ADULT EDUCATION

Colleges were one element in a trio of LEA services which developed separately from schools. The youth service worked across the school–college age range from the early to the late teens. It always aimed to include an educational element in its programme. Provision for youth service activities was made through grants to voluntary organisations and directly by the LEA in separate premises sometimes attached to comprehensive schools and occasionally to colleges. In some instances youth work was combined with teaching (FEU 1989a).

Although youth services were often part of the same LEA branch or department, links with further education and colleges were seldom strong. Once firmly established as an educational responsibility, the location of youth service provision within local authority services now varies. It may remain a part of the education service or be found grouped with leisure services. However, provision of all kinds is being reduced significantly due to lack of resources.

Adult education arrangements also vary from area to area. In some areas adult education is delivered through separate adult institutes and in other areas it is a department in further education colleges. Although often characterised as middle-class leisure provision, adult education has made a major contribution to improving adult literacy and employability by providing a way in to traditional further education for adults lacking confidence in their learning abilities (ALBSU 1992).

These three main elements in the post-school period, further education, the youth service and adult and continuing education, have often been seen as separate and independent services, with some notable exceptions. They have tended to work in isolation from each other. While each element has a specific role, however, all may be providing learning opportunities for the same individuals at different stages of their lives.

More recently there has been evidence that links are being built between them. All of them may provide continuing support during the transitions of young people and adults to and from education and employment. They need to become partners in offering a comprehensive service, to which individuals can have access according to their needs at appropriate stages in their lives, from adolescence to adulthood. However, the Further and Higher Education Act (1992) with its insistence on distinctions between vocational and non-vocational provision, will probably make cooperation between these three elements in post-school provision much more difficult.

THE TRAINING AGENCY INTERVENTION

During the early 1970s significant changes were beginning to take place in the labour market. Long-established heavy industries were in decline and service industries were growing. New technologies were changing the nature of jobs and the competences required for them. In rural areas more machinery on farms reduced labour requirements and stimulated a drift from the country into the towns. Information technology, travel and tourism and a variety of other new areas of work were being created.

Just over twenty years ago the government of the time became increasingly concerned about high levels of youth unemployment, particularly among low achievers, and about their inadequate preparation for the labour market. Considerable funds were redirected from LEAs to a separate agency, the then Manpower Services Commission.

The Commission was given responsibility for vocational preparation and instituted a variety of youth training schemes. Its single objective was vocational preparation. It was expected to buy in the most appropriate form of vocational training for different client groups from colleges and other appropriate trainers. Colleges had to compete for students and funds.

Mutual antagonism existed between the Commission and further education in the early days. Educationalists considered that it concentrated on vocational preparation to the virtual exclusion of other dimensions. A concentration on training outcomes resulted in too little attention to the quality and process of education. The Training Agency, as the Manpower Services Commission was renamed, considered that colleges were not meeting the education and training needs of the whole ability range, nor were they providing adequate preparation for work.

The setting up of a rival agency responsible for vocational preparation resulted in further education colleges reconsidering their roles and the ways in which they planned and evaluated their courses. The Agency was selective in its approach to the work-related non-advanced education and training it financed, requiring a structure with clear objectives, an instrumental approach to learning and performance criteria for evaluation (work-related non-advanced further education) (WRNAFE). As the government's training strategy and agenda was implemented, more funds were switched from LEAs to the Training Agency.

Colleges were confronted with the need to provide for a wider client group, particularly when delivering non-advanced further education and training for the agency. The Training Agency was the subject of the New Training Initiative at the beginning of the 1980s.

This initiative had three objectives, the improvement of:

- skill training;
- basic education and training for young people;
- training opportunities for adults.

The Training Agency has had many changes of name and function. Its original concerns covered all training and retraining, with a particular emphasis on young people leaving school and those who were unemployed. The 1988 Employment Act brought further changes, particularly in the balance between employers, trade unions, local authorities and further education. A Training Commission was set up and almost immediately disbanded. The Youth Training Board, the TVEI Steering Group and the Non-Advanced Further Education Steering Group were also disbanded. The Training, Education and Enterprise Directorate (TEED) of the Ministry of Employment was set up and local Training and Enterprise Councils (TECs) were formed.

TECS

While the basis of further education planning was being changed by the Education Reform Act (1988) the government made radical changes in the financing of employment training, some of which have already been mentioned. Various schemes financed by the TEED were discontinued. Much of the finance was reallocated to TECs, which were made responsible for the vocational preparation of young people and adults and for the rehabilitation and training of unemployed persons.

TECs were made responsible for employment training (ET), youth training (YT), WRNAFE, TVEI, Compacts and all the identified employment training needs of their areas. These employer-led councils have contracts with the Training Agency to plan and purchase education and training anywhere in their areas. There are now TECs in all areas of England and Wales, with boundaries that are seldom coterminous with the other bodies with which they work.

TECs, as major purchasers of training, are having a profound effect on the development plans of colleges. Councils all work independently and develop their own policies and procedures. Colleges have to become training organisations approved by councils and have to contract for work in competition with other training agencies. Some colleges have to deal with three or four TECs, all of whom may have different priorities and procedures. Such colleges are finding it difficult to develop coherent training programmes.

The Education Reform Act (1988)

This Act is the first of two introduced in the last five years to influence the management of further education. Designed to reduce the responsibilities of LEAs, it started to remove further education from their control. Major responsibilities for finance, management and college development were delegated to governors. Detailed requirements for articles of government and for responsibilities were outlined. In the last two years new governing boards of colleges have been coming to grips with their responsibilities and senior managers in colleges have been producing college development plans. The Further and Higher Education Act (1992) continues this reorganisation by setting up boards to manage incorporated colleges.

The White Paper

Changes were initiated by an earlier paper, *Managing Colleges Efficiently* (DES 1987). This introduced the concept of performance indicators, methods of calculating precise costs linked to student numbers and Training and Occupation Classification (TOC) categories on which to base student weightings, and influenced the approach adopted subsequently in the Education Reform Act (1988).

Subsequently the White Paper, *Education and Training for the 21st Century* (DES 1991), proposed to remove colleges from LEA, and indeed local elected member, control. New regional councils with responsibilities for funding and planning were to be set up under a central funding council. Funding arrangements which rewarded expansion were to be introduced.

A more controversial proposal was to separate vocational and non-vocational education for adults. The FEFC would only fund courses assumed to lead to vocational qualifications. Although consultation resulted in many objections to these proposals, particularly the artificial distinction being made between vocational and non-vocational adult education, the resulting Bill showed few modifications to the original proposals.

The White Paper had the following general aims:

- to establish a framework of vocational qualifications that are widely recognised and used, and that are relevant to the needs of the economy;
- to promote equal esteem for academic and vocational qualifications, and clearer and more accessible paths between them;
- to extend the range of services offered by school sixth forms and colleges, so that young people face fewer restrictions about what education or training they choose and where they take it up;
- to give TECs more scope to promote employer influence in education and mutual support between employers and education;
- to stimulate more young people to train, through the offer of a training credit;
- to promote links between schools and employers, to ensure that pupils gain a good understanding of the world of work before they leave school;

- to ensure that all young people get better information and guidance about the choices available to them at sixteen and as they progress through further education and training;
- to provide opportunities and incentives for young people to reach higher levels of attainment;
- to give colleges more freedom to expand their provision and respond more flexibly to the demands of their customers.

The White Paper Volume One went on to describe the current take-up of post-sixteen opportunities and the government's actions to date on each of the above aims.

The Higher and Further Education Act, based on the White Paper, was passed in the final days before the general election in 1992. It set up a Further Education Funding Council (FEFC) through which financial support for colleges is to be allocated. The Act completed the programme of reform set in motion at the end of the 1980s.

The recent history of further education has been one of continual change which has allowed colleges little time to absorb and respond to a series of policies and priorities. The following chapters describe some of the responses made to changing conditions.

Chapter 3

Recent influences

Colleges of further education have always catered for a wide age range of students and recognised the value of continued learning. The responsiveness of colleges to different educational and training demands has made them sensitive barometers of industrial and commercial change. Equally it is their relationships with employers and the labour market that has attracted increasing government attention.

Most recently colleges have been influenced by rapid changes in commerce and industry, together with high levels of unemployment, and by political and social interventions. An awareness of these influences is necessary to the understanding of the present state of further education and to the planning of its future development.

MAJOR GLOBAL AND INTERNATIONAL INFLUENCES

Major influences on further education range from shared global concerns through world and regional developments, national trends and policies to local community needs and pressures.

Vastly improved communications and transport systems have made everyone aware of interactions between regions and nations. For example, industrial development in the Far East has had a significant effect on industry in the United Kingdom. Regional developments, like the European Community (EC), also affect business and industry and education and training for employment. However, national preoccupations have the most influence, whether or not they reflect global, international and regional influences.

Major global influences Factors such as global warming, world population growth and ecological damage, to rain forests, for example, affect everyone. Topics such as energy use, the conservation of natural resources and feeding the world population are not just special studies but are becoming an integral part of college curricula and resource use (FEU 1992a). It is no longer possible to plan and offer further educational and training opportunities without paying attention to these influences. They have become a matter of concern to students of all ages. Government policies are being affected by them (White Paper 1990).

International concerns and relationships   These are having an increasing impact on individual countries. Education is having to prepare young people for living in a world where national interests are being subordinated to regional realities. People all over the world are expecting much more of the United Nations and of regional organisations, including the resolution of a wide range of social and economic problems as well as clashes between countries and ethnic groups. Changes such as new treaty obligations in the EC, political and labour market changes in Eastern Europe, commercial developments in the Far East, all have their influence on the labour market and on further education and vocational training.

Vocational preparation for a wide range of employment has to take into account international trends and developments. For example, there has to be increased attention to the culture and practices of other countries in management training and business studies. World standards are now expected in education and training. The curriculum is expected to improve linguistic skills in the native language and to increase abilities to communicate in other languages and compete for employment in other European countries (FEU 1986, 1989c).

A recent EC study of student choice has shown that a very high percentage of students from member countries place the United Kingdom as their first choice for education and training. Among other reasons for their choice, the value of learning English predominates. United Kingdom students, on the other hand, seldom choose other countries, mainly because of their lack of other languages. There is an increasing exchange of students between EC countries and these exchanges may be expected to influence further educational provision more and more in the future. The time is now long past when a local technical college could concentrate on training for a local industry. Although meeting the needs of local commerce and industry are primary concerns, many local firms are operating in other countries and some are linked with multi-national companies. Thus education and training have to take into account both national and international practices and technical developments.

NATIONAL INFLUENCES

Some national influences on further education result from the political character of the times. Others stem from the effects of new technologies on industry and commerce and from the aspirations of potential students. The effective further education college has always been responsive to these influences on its work (FEU 1987a; 1987b; 1989d; 1989e).

However, government policies have been, and are, characterised by a distrust of the education system, a reliance on short-term solutions, the application of industrial and commercial management methods to solve social and educational problems and a belief in the universal benefits of market forces. The effects of these policies on the management and financing of colleges and on the support of students is discussed elsewhere.

Industrial and commercial changes   New patterns of employment in business and industry now require different qualifications and skills. Major industries, like coal, steel and heavy engineering, have declined, with consequent effects on employment prospects. The mechanisation of agriculture has changed the pattern of rural employment and encouraged a drift of population to urban areas. New technologies and new machinery have reduced the demand for labour as profits are seen to flow from low labour costs. The change from a productive to a service economy has required the introduction of new technologies, particularly information technology, in management and business.

At the same time, however, there has been little investment in new patterns of employment, such as job sharing. More recently a recession has increased job losses and decreased investment in training. As a result, preparation for the labour market of the twenty-first century is patchy and limited. Further education has made a significant contribution to the education and retraining of those made redundant and those who need to learn new skills. To respond effectively colleges need up-to-date market intelligence. However, education and training have not yet produced the competences and levels of skill that are necessary in a flexible work-force.

While both the government and industry have criticised further education there has been a difference in emphasis. The government's line has been a return to the basics taught by traditional didactic methods. The CBI (1989), on the other hand, while wanting to see a general improvement in linguistic, communication and numeracy skills, recognises that modern-day conditions require other skills as well. Employers see problem-solving and working in groups as essential outcomes of education and training. These capabilities are not always developed by traditional methods or within specific vocational training programmes.

Employers Employers have been asked to increase their involvement in further education and training. The government has taken action to recruit managers in industry and commerce in a number of ways. They form a majority on the new funding council, on bodies developing and accrediting National Vocational Qualifications (NVQs) (FEU 1989f), on Training and Enterprise Councils (TECs) and on the governing bodies of colleges. Thus they have the major influence on funding and priorities.

It is too soon to judge the influence of employers on colleges, as they are learning about their responsibilities as a result of changing legislation. The management teams in TECs, colleges and training agencies are also at the early stage of developing their contribution.

Equal opportunities Many of the changes in the student population have been stimulated by the introduction of equal opportunities in education and employment. Equal opportunities legislation and practices have had a significant influence on colleges. Although the last decade has seen a considerable increase in recruitment, some groups remain under-represented, in general or in particular vocational areas, in further education. These include women, members of ethnic minorities, those who are disabled and other groups not previously seeking or gaining access to further education.

The national curriculum   The final years of the 1980s saw the introduction of a national curriculum for pupils from five to sixteen years of age. Standard assessments of achievements at the ages of seven, eleven and sixteen are being introduced (Education Reform Act 1988). The immediate effect on further education has been slight. But as pupils leave school, having followed the national curriculum for all of their school life, colleges will have a much clearer picture of the prior learning of their students. The links being forged between the national curriculum and General National Vocational Qualifications (GNVQs) will create a closer relationship between school performance and further and continuing education standards. It should be easier to provide the continuity between pre- and post-school education that is essential for the effective use of resources.

REGIONAL INFLUENCES

In addition to the national trends there have been and are strong regional influences on the work of colleges. The pattern of courses and qualifications they provide has reflected established regional industries such as steel and coal. Even where traditional industries remain, working practices have had to change to take into account new technologies and plant. For example, the decline of the mining industry followed by the introduction of new highly technical industries has changed the pattern of further education and training needs in South Wales. Other areas, where heavy industries such as shipbuilding have declined or ceased, have had to attract new enterprises and develop a work-force with new skills. Japanese industry in the north-east of England is one example. Regional tourism with its associated service-based employment has also been a major new development. The college response has been to work with employers to develop appropriate courses in colleges and in the work-place.

DEMOGRAPHIC CHANGE

Changes in the size of youth and young adult age groups in the population have had a significant effect on colleges. Education and training for those who were demobilised resulted in high post-war admission rates. Later, as the children from post-war marriages left school, encouragement to seek vocational training resulted in increased admission rates. Subsequent surges in the youth population have also brought peak admission years.

Cyclical variations in the size of age groups continue to occur in a generally falling birth-rate. However, although youth age groups have reduced in size, the numbers of adults applying to colleges has steadily increased, so that the age distribution of the college student population is similar to that of the population as a whole.

Young people and young adults   Many young people see the college of further education as providing a more attractive and adult alternative to the sixth form. This has resulted in an increase in the size of general studies departments providing 'O' and 'A' level courses as well as other general educational qualifications. Young people are now faced with four options at the age of sixteen, although not all exist in all areas. These are to:

- continue in the sixth form of their school;
- attend a sixth form college;
- attend a tertiary college;
- attend a college of further education.

There are a number of reasons why young people choose to enter further education after leaving school. Some of them are that colleges provide:

- an attractive alternative for taking 'O' and 'A' level GCSE courses;
- a wider range of 'O' and 'A' level subjects and combinations of subjects;
- a wider range of post-sixteen vocational qualifications which are increasingly valued;
- an increasing number of youth training initiatives.

It is unfortunate that post-sixteen educational opportunities have to be taken immediately on leaving secondary school. Many young people are not ready to profit from them. If the sixteen to eighteen-plus entitlement to further education could be grant-aided at any age, results might be impressive.

Changes in industry and commerce are demanding a work-force with a wider range of vocational qualifications and competences. A variety of new courses and modules have been developed to meet these demands and attract more students. However, there is a wider difference in the opportunities available in urban and rural areas where transport difficulties add to the lack of choice (FEU 1988a, 1988b).

Although youth age groups have been decreasing in size in recent years, youth training initiatives have attempted to increase the involvement of the 40 per cent of the group who, in the past, did not usually seek education or training after leaving school. However, a percentage of this group are disenchanted with the education system and as yet further education has been relatively unsuccessful in attracting them into colleges.

Adult admission From the immediate post-war until the mid-1970s the sixteen to nineteen age group formed the majority of the student population except where colleges were responsible for adult education. In recent years the age distribution of students in colleges without adult education responsibilities has become closer to population norms. This has been the result of a new emphasis on adult retraining, of an increased number of women preparing to return to employment, and of meeting the needs of members of minority ethnic groups.

All these trends have been associated with greater attention to facilitating the access of potential students to colleges. Access is a word used in three different ways in further and higher education:

1 in a general sense to describe better and more appropriate opportunities for students and thus to make access to college easier;
2 in association with disadvantage where 'access funds' are made available in further and higher education to support individual students over the age of eighteen;
3 in a specific sense when colleges provide 'access courses' to enable students to gain access to further and higher education programmes.

Family patterns and aspirations have resulted in more women seeking employment and preparing for it through further education. Not only have colleges had to provide for a more adult population but they have had to consider the particular needs of single parents and working mothers for assistance with child care. Crèche and nursery facilities have become more common.

The existence of ethnic groups in the community as a result of immigration in previous decades has brought other needs for further and continuing education. Raising educational achievements through access courses and developing English as a second language skills have been two outcomes. Retaining and sustaining the cultural identities have also been important factors in the nature of effective provision for such students (FEU 1988c; FEU/REPLAN 1989; FEU 1989g). Colleges have also been responding to a wide range of other community needs including those of the active retirement group which is growing in size in the final decade of the century.

OTHER INFLUENCES

National qualifications A tangle of different qualifications granted by different bodies grew up in the post-war years. More recently two forms of national qualification have been developed: NVQs, related to specific employment sectors, and GNVQs, concerned with general education, training and employability skills (FEU 1989h). To achieve a level of qualification involves the acquisition of both knowledge and skills. Theoretical and academic knowledge is important but not sufficient for qualification. Competence has to be demonstrated (FEU 1989i).

In each employment sector, levels of competence have been, or are being, agreed between employers, professional and vocational assessment bodies and educational and training agencies. The initial levels, particularly of GNVQs, are being related to levels achieved at sixteen by school leavers following the national curriculum. A particular feature of NVQs is that they are intended to take account of and build on prior learning (FEU/UDACE 1992).

Although some colleges have yet to reconsider their traditional attitudes and practices, many others are developing new patterns of organisation and provision (FEU 1991d). The introduction of NVQs has resulted in a move to more flexible models of provision. Prior learning is being credited, and the introduction of modular courses is allowing students to choose an individual programme which builds on previous achievements (FEU 1992b). The ability to accumulate credits for completing different modules successfully and changed patterns of assessment are also influencing the ways in which further education and training are delivered, particularly in Scotland (FEU 1992c).

AN ENTERPRISE CULTURE

The enterprise culture is here to stay as long as the present government continues to be re-elected. It is therefore important that all those working in further and continuing education recognise and understand the international, national and regional influences affecting their work. They also need to know their institutions and understand how they work (FESC 1991). The strengths and weaknesses of the enterprise culture must be recognised (FEU/DTI 1989).

There has been and there is bound to be conflict between educational aspirations and the enterprise culture. Colleges will no longer have the protection of the LEA and of elected local representatives of the community. They may become more vulnerable to commercial competition and niche marketing. One example of such an approach is provided by a hospital which has become a training organisation for medical secretaries. It can afford to pay trainees a basic wage, provide a wide range of work experience, develop personal and social skills within the organisation and be commercially viable.

Market forces have both positive and negative effects on individuals and further education institutions. Negative effects include personal isolation and alienation from the ethos and a loss of a sense of direction and purpose. Positive effects may result in new staff solidarity in the face of competition, a creative responsiveness to change and more effective marketing and use of resources. The direction of attention towards professional accountability and quality control is a positive outcome for any system. The market-place approach forces further and continuing education to examine attitudes to success and failure.

Two particular issues are the achievement of social justice in the face of immediate market imperatives and the equitable management of the system. The new funding systems and the increased entrepreneurial activities of colleges are making some aspects of their work vulnerable. Recent influences have not been on the side of those with greatest needs but of those with greatest economic potential.

One of the depressing aspects of the government's approach to education in the 1980s has been the assumption that professional opinions are of little value. Troublesome union minorities have been taken to represent responsible educational judgement. Consultation has often been a pretence with little intention of taking notice of any other than political considerations. Taken together with a continued attack on local government, planning for further education has been seriously hampered by many of the steps intended to improve it.

EQUAL OPPORTUNITIES

Colleges have become free-standing competing businesses whose priorities will be determined by who finances them. It is difficult to see who will be in a position to ensure that:

- a similar range of opportunities is available nationally;
- all regional and local needs are met;
- adequate provision is made for minorities and the hard to educate.

There is no doubt that the Further Education Funding Council is charged with an oversight of the range of opportunities available. Of all the minority needs, the Council is charged only with securing that proper assessments of the needs of individuals with disabilities and learning difficulties are made and that provision is made for them. The Council's Circulars recognise these responsibilities.

If colleges are not socially responsible, and do not attend to community needs of all kinds, who will attend to them? The new system is based on the belief that market forces will automatically provide for all needs. In practice they do not always result in equity and an even distribution of opportunities, nor do they always cater adequately for minority needs. Who in the future will have an overview to ensure that the educational and training needs of all sectors of the community are met?

Chapter 4

Potential students

The demand for further education is increasing as young people and adults of all ages are looking to colleges to enhance their employment prospects and their quality of life. Not only are more young people being sponsored through youth training schemes, continued unemployment is also persuading many of them to remain in full-time education after the age of sixteen. At the same time more adults are looking to further education for vocational preparation and up-dating (DE/NIACE/REPLAN 1989; FEU/REPLAN 1989b, 1990).

However, there remain many people who do not see themselves as potential learners. A combination of unsatisfactory experiences in school and of disadvantaged social conditions leads to a lack of confidence in themselves and in educational institutions. Many persuade themselves that they are outside a system which has little to offer them; a system which is not always aware of the importance of attracting disaffected and disenchanted learners into further education (FEU/NIACE 1992).

It is important to consider the range of potential students. Some changes in the student population have already been mentioned. The purpose of this chapter is to describe the diversity of students and student needs in the current college population. It may be that legislative and economic pressures will cause colleges to restrict what they offer but it is important that they do not lose sight of the whole range of needs they ought, if possible, to meet.

POPULATION PARAMETERS

The number of students with different needs may change but the diversity of those needs is unlikely to do so. This range of needs can best be illustrated by setting out a number of factors which staff should take into account in their delivery of education and training of quality. These parameters of the student population include the:

- age range of students from sixteen-plus to sixty-plus;
- ability range of students;
- range of student achievement levels;
- different rates and styles of learning of students;
- variety of prior experience of students;
- range of different student social, economic and cultural backgrounds;
- range of student aspirations and educational needs.

The range of student needs has important implications for the ways in which colleges deliver further education and training. They have to provide programmes, at different times, in different locations, to meet different employer and student requirements.

The age range   This starts from the end of the compulsory school period and covers both late adolescent and adult learning needs. At the other end of the range it includes not only the years of employment but also those of active retirement (FEU/REPLAN 1989c).

The ability range   The existence of a higher education system by no means limits the range of ability in further education. Many students may prefer a more vocational orientation to their studies. Others may be lacking in confidence and not be aware of their potential.
   Two other developments attract students with higher academic potential: franchise arrangements with universities for first-year undergraduate work and highly technical short courses.

The range of attainment   Although ability and achievement are linked, limited achievements do not necessarily imply limited ability. Further education is a field where assumptions of competence based on academic attainments are least justified.

The range of rates and styles of learning   A wider range of students will bring with them much more varied learning skills and experiences. These different styles and rates demand that staff have a thorough understanding of the learning process and use their knowledge in individual programme planning (FEU 1990b).

The variety of prior learning   The introduction of the national curriculum may result in an easier accreditation of the prior learning of school leavers entering further education. However, older students in mid-career may bring much more varied learning skills and experiences to their further education and staff will need to recognise and respect this. For example, women may have developed highly effective management skills while bringing up their children.

Prior educational achievement alone should not determine expectations. One of the challenges faced by staff when levels of prior achievement vary widely is how to respond to students who have reached different levels of competence.

The range of social, economic and cultural backgrounds
Further education is a melting-pot in which different family, cultural and educational backgrounds begin to share common experiences based on vocational aspirations. Variations in background and values have to be recognised, even where they have no obvious relevance to the curriculum (FEU 1988c).

The range of student needs   There is no limit to the range of needs which further education can and should meet. Vocational preparation including necessary qualifications is an obvious need. Gaining access to education via a bridging experience is another common need. Less obvious are the needs generated by new legislation or marketing practices.

The actual and potential students whose needs these parameters define fall into two broad groups, with an ill-defined boundary between them: young people at the beginning of their adult working lives, and adults of all ages.

Young people

Young people leaving school may or may not have made decisions about their futures. Some may need to acquire academic qualifications, others to taste and test vocational possibilities. The development into adulthood evident in the late teens requires an education programme giving due weight to personal and social development. All such students may need guidance, counselling and careers advice (FEU 1988d, 1988e). Support services to provide them will be necessary to help young people to plan wisely and to enable them to sustain their motivation and application.

It is evident, in practice, that young people enter further education with widely varied levels of maturity. They may have chosen further education instead of remaining in school, but they are equally likely to vote with their feet and leave if it does not meet their current needs.

School leavers

The further education and training of school leavers has always been a major concern of colleges. Age groups are now decreasing in size and will only increase slightly in the late 1990s. School leavers vary in their needs and in their motivation and a number of sub-groups are evident. One traditional group consists of school leavers with acceptable school achievements, who choose to seek vocational qualifications. Another group of leavers choose post-'O' level academic courses not available in schools. Since the 1960s student status and the more adult atmosphere of colleges has proved a powerful attraction to many school leavers as an alternative to the traditional sixth form. Enabling young people to retake 'O' levels and to take 'A' level courses became a major college activity. Both groups tend to be well motivated and in the past they have enabled colleges to maintain standards and meet the requirements of examining boards and professions.

Students from different ethnic groups

Another group for whom colleges had to reappraise their provision was that of young people from the increasing variety of ethnic, cultural and linguistic backgrounds who were applying for further education opportunities. The background of the youth population for which colleges are now expected to make provision has widened significantly in the second half of the twentieth century.

Youth employment training

The end of the 1970s and the early 1980s brought an increase in employment-funded training. Colleges competed for youth training opportunities and thus recruited a group sometimes less motivated towards educational and vocational proficiency. For many of these young people school had been a place to leave as soon as possible. Their achievements were often limited and their attitudes to learning far from positive. The introduction of these students caused colleges to reconsider their curricula and methods and make a sustained effort to provide a wider range of educational opportunities.

Students with disabilities and learning difficulties

At about the same time the Warnock Report drew attention to the very limited post-school opportunities available to young people with disabilities and learning difficulties. Although there was some provision in specialist colleges, there were very few opportunities in local colleges. As a result of that Report and the efforts of pioneers more and more colleges began to make arrangements to accommodate a wider range of students with varied learning difficulties.

The introduction of a philosophy of integration also brought pressure to provide living and working opportunities in the community for young people with disabilities and learning difficulties. The further education college was seen as the best setting to facilitate integration and competence in the community (FEU 1990d). By the time the Education Reform Act (1988) was implemented, local education authorities (LEAs) and colleges were expected to include provision for students with disabilities and learning difficulties in their strategic and development plans.

The FEFC is charged with seeing that the further education and training needs of these students are assessed and that colleges make provision to meet the needs of these students. The Council's Circulars (for example, FEFC 92/09) draw the attention of colleges to their responsibilities for this aspect of their work.

Adult students

Although in the post-war period the needs of youth groups received a degree of priority, the traditional provision of vocational preparation and second-chance education for adults did not cease. Colleges continued to offer opportunities to acquire skills and qualifications. But new groups have been added to the adult population of colleges, some as a result of the limited incentives now being offered (FEU/REPLAN 1989c).

Although many adult students have to finance their own further education and training, a number of forms of assistance are available. Adult education may provide a supported re-entry to learning. For those who need it there will be support from adult literacy and numeracy schemes. Employers also fund training which enhances personal and vocational skills. One example of this approach is the investment made by the Ford Company. Other initiatives include:

- *Access Funds* which are government grants to colleges to facilitate the access of students over the age of eighteen to education. They may be used in cases of hardship and where the individual is disabled;
- *Employment Training Grants* which are made available to adults who are unemployed to enable them to acquire vocational skills to enhance their employment prospects (FEU 1990c);
- *LEA Discretionary Awards* which still continue to be made in some circumstances but are becoming increasingly rare.

New technology

Changes in society, industry and business are resulting in new demands from a wide range of different adult groups. These result from new employment practices replacing those which have remained the same for generations. They also arise where traditional industries are no longer viable and are being replaced by less labour-intensive specialist and service businesses. With new technologies and working practices, jobs have changed and disappeared and new ones have been created. With the rapid changes taking place, retraining may be necessary three or four times in a working life. Vocational training is no longer for life.

Another effect of new technologies and working practices has been the development of transferable skills and of the multi-skilled worker. A large number of similar skills are now common to different crafts, trades and professions. Also, in small businesses and in maintenance work, costs prevent the employment of a wide variety of different tradesmen. Shared training and multi-skill development are two current aspects of adult further education.

The increasing number of small businesses, encouraged by the enterprise initiative, create education and training needs particularly in the fields of management training and information technology skills. As a result of information technology, an increasing number of employees are undertaking computer-based work at home. One LEA is now using this system for most of its administration. This has advantages for men and women who prefer to work from home, for those with disabilities and for others who prefer flexible working.

Unemployment

Economic recessions in the 1970s and 1980s resulted in periods of high unemployment which are continuing into the 1990s. One answer to the problem was seen to be retraining, which became a Department of Employment priority. Colleges were expected to develop a new range of courses. Funding arrangements for training meant that colleges competed with other training organisations for resources. Unemployed people represent a large group of potential students who need personal as well as vocational educational opportunities (FEU 1989n).

Equal opportunities

Over the same period a developing emphasis on equal opportunities resulted in increased demands for further education and training from other groups, including women, members of ethnic minority groups and those with disabilities and learning difficulties. In all instances attempts had to be made to make education and training accessible (FEU 1990c).

A wide variety of new ethnic groups have established families in this country in the past four decades and new groups continue to arrive. For some, English was a second language not normally spoken in the home. For others, previous educational experience had been limited. The educational achievements of children during the school period could also be limited and steps had to be taken to remedy this in the post-school period. Young people and adults turned to further and higher education for help. Access courses and other arrangements were instituted to enable individuals to profit from further education (FEU 1987c).

A large number of women have been entering the labour market in the last two decades. There are a number of reasons for this, including equal opportunities policies which encourage employers to offer more jobs to women, and women themselves seeking status through gaining paid employment. Perhaps as significant have been political and commercial inducements which raise expectations of higher standards of living, which in turn demand two incomes to achieve and maintain them. Part-time employment opportunities have increased markedly. Women entering or returning to work have sought preparation through both non-vocational and vocational further education. As a result colleges have been providing for them not only through the courses on offer but also through 'return to learning' access courses and child care arrangements to facilitate their attendance (FEU 1990e; EOC/FEU 1989; FEU 1989i).

The balance of the college student population is changing, with adult students being in the majority and women forming about half the population. Changes in the age range have made attention to the parameters already outlined more important, particularly the accreditation of prior learning, and have also revealed other student needs to be taken into account.

Recurrent education

Recurrent education has now become a feature of the lives of many adults. The need to upgrade, to retrain and to maximise competence has brought this home to employers. But there are also raised expectations in society. Many individuals wish to develop their working lives and careers by increasing skills and qualifications. Colleges are becoming aware of the recurrent student and the implications of such students for policies and practices.

Help is often required by individuals to sort out possibilities and plan their career development. Prior learning needs to be recognised and built on and the college programme has to include elements attractive to regular and recurrent students. The availability of guidance, counselling and career development services is becoming vital.

Student sponsorship

Sponsorship of individual students has always existed but contractual sponsorship of groups and particular courses has brought new issues to the surface. A variety of new terms have emerged, such as 'clients' and 'customers', to describe college relationships with sponsors and students. But important questions arise: to whom is the college ultimately responsible, the student or the sponsor? What rights does the student have when a sponsor is negotiating and paying for a programme.

If, for example, sponsors enter into a contract with the college, they expect certain student outcomes to be delivered. The college also has responsibilities to the individual students it enrols. All is well when sponsor and student interests coincide. What is less clear is what happens when they do not. Individuals undertake education and training for different purposes and reasons.

Although personal motivation is not always easy to distinguish from student motivation associated with commercial sponsorship, it is necessary to be clear as to who is selecting students for particular courses and modules and how much choice sponsored students might have.

Some of these concerns will be related to the financing of further education and training in future. While those who pay are entitled to negotiate desired outcomes, it is far less certain that they should determine the processes by which they are achieved. Sponsor and student entitlements need to be defined so that both parties and the college are clear about what is being paid for and who is responsible for the quality of the educational process.

The increased commercial and agency responsibility for the sponsorship of further education and training could have a restrictive effect on college practices and student choice. Individual colleges, without the backing of LEAs, may be vulnerable to pressures which promote training at the expense of education and commercial interests at the expense of student opportunities (FEU 1992d).

Training Enterprise Councils (TECs) and their priorities

Because of the funds being allocated to TECs they will have a strong influence on youth training and adult retraining. In future TECs may sponsor students who are on:

- Employment training (ET);
- Youth training (YT);
- Work-related non-advanced further education (WRNAFE);
- Technical, Vocational Educational Initiative (TVEI);
- Other schemes.

They will also be responsible for the administration of training credits, discussed elsewhere, which are likely to be used increasingly in association with youth training programmes.

TECs will be expected to identify local employment needs and the training to meet them. It remains to be seen how their priorities relate to those of the new funding councils and whether colleges have clear messages about the student groups for which they are expected to provide.

Inclusiveness

Increased participation has been a major objective of many colleges. One of the implications of this objective is inclusiveness (FEU 1992e). The concept of inclusiveness embodies a sensitive response to the needs of students:

- from ethnic and other minority groups;
- returning to learning;
- with disabilities and learning difficulties;
- whose individual needs include attention to variations in their pace and style of learning (FEU 1988f);
- unfamiliar with continuing education.

The inclusive college also has a number of other characteristics which include:

- the recognition and accreditation of prior learning;
- the provision of bridging activities to facilitate access to regular programmes;
- the negotiation of individual learning programmes with students;
- the provision of opportunities to learn in a variety of ways, including distance learning, open learning and student work-shops;
- the availability of learning support.

In seeking to provide education of quality the college is concerned not only with the nature of the learning but also with the social contexts in which it takes place. Responsibility for its students includes providing counselling, guidance and personal support as well as a wide range of services to support individual learning.

Where further education is narrowly conceived, every new additional group is seen as creating potentially disruptive precedents. The wider the population basis on which the college programme is initially planned, the easier it is to accommodate variations in demand and learning needs.

There has been a tradition of staff and students being valued according to the academic or technical level of the work they do.

But an effective equity policy, for example, values the potential of all individuals and invests resources in redressing disadvantages. Economic pressures may now lead to students being valued according to the resources they bring to the college.

When a college adopts inclusiveness this policy will need to be reflected in its development and business plans which should embody clear statements about how inclusiveness is to be made effective and the nature and time-scale of funding to increase access and inclusiveness. The college will also need to ensure that it has an appropriate organisation and management structure to implement a policy of inclusiveness.

The idea of college inclusiveness assumes that all learners are of equal value. It implies that college organisation facilitates access and participation and that marketing is concerned with both commercial and community needs. Inclusiveness is made much harder to achieve when admission to programmes excludes large sectors of the community.

The majority of potential students want further education and training opportunities of high quality but of a level appropriate to their needs. Since well over a third of the potential student population has been neglected in the past, it would be unfortunate if new, incorporated further education businesses and those responsible for funding repeated that error.

Chapter 5

The college response – the elements

Colleges of further education have changed in response to major employment and education legislation and have had to develop relationships with a range of agencies. In addition to examining bodies, employers and industrial training boards, with whom they have worked closely in the past, colleges have had to build up their contacts with the Training Agency, in its many guises, and more recently with Training and Enterprise Councils (TECs). They have also been subject to pressures from employers and students. This chapter discusses how colleges have been reacting to the complex web of demands made on them in the recent past.

Recently colleges have been in different stages of transformation to independent businesses. Some have reorganised and changed their practices and are well on the way to a coherent response to change (FEU 1988j). Others are still clinging to traditional practices. The descriptions of procedural changes which follow represent a relatively optimistic picture.

Changes have taken place in five broad areas;

- management;
- organisation;
- procedures;
- teaching and learning strategies;
- staff development.

Management, including new patterns of college management, and *organisation*, concerned with new faculty structures and cross-college facilities and services, will be discussed in the next chapter.

PROCEDURAL CHANGES

These changes have involved planning, resource management, admission procedures, marketing and staff development, as well as the development of different styles of management (FEU 1988k; FEU 1989j).

Planning

Local education authorities (LEAs) have supported the development of their colleges of further education in a variety of ways. Administratively the majority have had a further education section, often also responsible for adult education and the youth service. In practice further education sections provided colleges with administrative services of different kinds. While these sections may have had few planned or regular contacts with other administrative sections within the education department, they usually maintained links with a wide variety of outside bodies. LEA management of further and continuing education varied from the enlightened to the ineffective. Until comparatively recently very few authorities had their own professional advisors for this phase of education.

Professional advice to the authority and colleges mainly came from Regional Further Education Advisory Committees and from HM Inspectorate. Colleges have always maintained links with employers, many of whom acted as members of advisory committees for different vocational areas. Most authorities had plans for the development of their further education provision and effective colleges have always planned ahead.

Principals of colleges were expected to be entrepreneurs and their professional advancement was often based on expansion and the development of higher-level work. There was a general trend to upgrade the level of work since the higher the level of academic or technical work, the higher the salaries of the staff concerned. Higher-status provision brought higher funding. This enabled some colleges to progress to advanced technology and polytechnic status and finally to becoming universities.

When most course provision was determined by a range of professional and technical bodies, strategic planning and development appeared less important. The LEA role was largely confined to endorsing college initiatives and ensuring that provision was adequate to cover community needs. Elected members of the LEA formed the majority on governing bodies of colleges and largely reflected local authority views. Planning depended on the extent to which LEAs and senior management teams of colleges made it a priority. LEAs were only required to have strategic plans when the Education Reform Act (1988) was implemented.

The development of work-related further education, youth training and employment training in the early 1980s, funded by the Department of Employment through its Training Agency, brought with it a demand for effective planning. Courses had to be designed for students, many of whom had limited educational achievements and uncertain motivation. They had to:

• provide appropriate vocational preparation;
• have a clearly defined set of behavioural objectives;
• achieve agreed outcomes measured in terms of skills and competences.

This relatively low-level work was financially attractive to colleges. If they wished to compete for funds, they had to become approved training organisations. Their course planning and curriculum development procedures had to be improved. Staff also had to learn to teach a different range of students.

Over the same period colleges were being encouraged to expand while at the same time experiencing cuts in their funding. Commercial and marketing skills were developed. Answers to the paradox of more provision with fewer resources were seen to lie in college-generated income and self-financed full-cost courses.

The effective competition of colleges in the market-place, which new legislation is intended to promote, will depend on good planning and resource management (FEU 1989k). It is now the responsibility of governors and senior managers to assess the college resources, make themselves aware of education and training demands in the local communities, and plan what can be offered.

In the process they have to find answers to questions like:

• What are the demands being made on the college?
• What resources are available to the college?
• What are the main priorities in the college plan?
• What core entitlement to all students can the college afford?
• Within college priorities what resources can be found to make that entitlement as broad as possible?

Reference has already been made to the concept of inclusiveness (see previous chapter). The narrower and more exclusive the criteria for admission to further education, the more difficult it is to include provision for educational needs which may be different from those which it is planned to meet. It is important to recognise that the wider the population basis for planning, and the more inclusive the admission criteria, the easier it will be to accommodate different students' needs and variation in learning styles, rates of learning and individual abilities.

Resource management

Resource management was originally a fairly simple matter of allocating available resources from a single source – the LEA – to a group of competing and relatively autonomous college departments. Now it is more complex, with finance coming from many sources, including income generated by college departments and its approved training organisation (FESC 1988; FESC 1991b). Prudent budgeting is essential as the penalties for overspending are severe. Excess spending is doubly penalised. The sum concerned has not only to be cut from the current budget but any overspending is carried forward and decreases the budget for the next financial year.

College organisation is becoming more complex. Departmental autonomy is decreasing and there is closer collaboration between departments or faculties. There is a new emphasis on curriculum teams drawn from a number of departments and on the development of programmes to which departments contribute modules. There is an increase in the quantity and quality of common cross-college facilities and services such as libraries, media resource centres and student counselling services.

Budgeting and resource allocation procedures are now more complicated. They have to take into account who provides the resources, the entitlement of departments to self-generating funds and shared responsibilities for student programmes. Governors and senior managers are now having to take responsibility for budgetary matters previously supported, informed and managed by LEA-elected members and officers.

Marketing

The traditional pattern of student recruitment has depended on the production of a prospectus by the college and the application by potential individual students for places on courses described in that prospectus, or on contracts with large employers for day-release education and training. Although there is a marketing element in that approach, competition for funds and students and the need to generate income demand a more active approach to recruitment. Marketing now involves knowledge of potential demands, flexible publicity and high-quality information aimed at employers and potential students (FEU/FESC 1985; FESC 1989; FEU 1990f).

There is now competition between schools and colleges for the post-sixteen student and this will be increased by new proposals for funding. Schools will now be able to include technical options in their range of post-sixteen courses. Where school sixth forms are struggling to survive it will be vital for young people to get independent information and guidance and be made aware of the opportunities offered by further education colleges, particularly those which schools cannot offer. A number of introductory courses have been mounted for students who have chosen a field but need to explore it before making vocational choices. These include traditional foundation courses in art and design, the Diploma of Vocational Education and the BTec Certificate.

Marketing through well-prepared information relevant to particular groups is now a common feature of effective practice. This involves a study of potential students, their needs and their employment potential, and decisions about what programmes to offer. It requires an active knowledge of the particular field of commerce or industry and of what employers are seeking for their staff. The form of the prospectus can make what is on offer more of less accessible. In some areas this may involve printing information in more than one language.

More recently, attention has been given to the development of course packages based on a study of local needs. Sometimes these have been devised by colleges to inform groups of professionals and employees about the requirements of new legislation. For example, people have been required to undertake training to handle pesticides or deal with other health and safety legislation.

At other times these education and training packages have been devised with particular employers, or sectors of commerce and industry, to update staff in new technologies or new procedures. In both instances the college offering has not been devised solely by the educator but has resulted from collaboration with employers (FEU 1992f).

The recruitment of students from overseas has become a growing feature in college marketing. The attraction of further education in the United Kingdom for students from other European Community countries has already been mentioned (see Chapter 3). There is a potential for development to which specific marketing is now being directed.

Some outreach work takes place with youth groups, and with parents in adult education, to recruit to further education those with unsatisfactory school experiences, reluctant learners and those disenchanted with the education system. There is also some evidence of schools and colleges working together on adult literacy projects (FEU/REPLAN 1989d).

A further aspect of marketing, to be discussed later, is the introduction of quality assurance. The marketing of courses or modules is facilitated when the quality of what is offered is consistent and high. This quality should be judged not only by outcomes but also by the processes by which those outcomes are achieved. Effective marketing involves the college in developing easily recognisable quality criteria (FEU 1991c).

Access to college

The various ways in which the term 'access' is used have been described in Chapter 3. Access to college is concerned with the ways in which potential students are made aware of what is on offer, how they are welcomed to the college, and the guidance and counselling available to support their learning.

Both pre-admission information and admission procedures should be sensitive to problems of access. Some colleges arrange evenings where adults can receive individual guidance in confidence. A number of colleges have been very successful in making themselves more accessible to potential students. A warm welcome, clear signposting, sensitive guidance and the availability of learning support are among important indicators of accessibility.

A number of initiatives facilitate access to college. One is the Pick-Up Programme (FEU 1990g) to revive learning skills and gain entry to vocational qualification courses. Access courses and bridging courses are available to prepare individuals for entry to academic and technical courses (FEU 1987).

Counselling, guidance and tutoring

All the changes in the student population and in admission procedures have brought with them new responsibilities to provide student support services. Careers guidance in schools has had to be linked with course choice or individual study programmes in college. Many students require guidance and support to sustain their educational efforts. Without a well-organised guidance and support system other individual students may lack a coherent programme of studies which ensures continuity and progression in their acquisition of skills and competences. Learning support, discussed later, and personal tutoring have also been introduced to help individuals.

Not only do students need support services on admission and during their time in college but they also need help with planning their exit from them. Increasing attention is being given to careers and personal guidance at the completion of a period of further education in collaboration with the careers service.

Admission

Admission arrangements could be kept simple when well-motivated applicants, with recognised pre-qualifications, were applying for a finite number of discrete courses. But the numbers of such applicants are decreasing. The wider range of students seeking access to further education requires appropriate admission procedures which include an assessment of their potential and learning needs.

By the time the national curriculum has been taught to them throughout their secondary schooling, school leavers applying for further education will have had their achievement levels recorded in a standard form. As a result, admission procedures for this group may be relatively simple when linked with careers guidance in schools.

However, for the majority of adults applying for admission there may be limited records of previous educational and training experiences. Because levels of school achievement are rarely maintained in the absence of continuing education it may be difficult to assess prior learning. Nevertheless this will have to be assessed before designing individual programmes to achieve National Vocational Qualifications (NVQs) and General National Vocational Qualifications (GNVQs) (FEU 1992b).

Admission procedures should ensure that:

- appropriate individual counselling and guidance is available;
- students receive information about available means of financial support for their studies;
- applicants find relevant courses of study;
- students get appropriate opportunities for personal development;
- attention is drawn to student needs which are not being met and education opportunities the college ought to be offering.

Teaching and learning strategies

New strategies, associated with course and curriculum development, have been developed as a result of the admission of new student groups with a wider variety of educational and training needs. Curriculum development (FEU 1988h) has brought with it an increased emphasis on student participation so that didactic instruction is being replaced, with managed learning delivered not only in the college but elsewhere.

Staff are working in situations outside colleges in factories, business premises, prisons and other institutions. They are providing distance teaching and are working collaboratively with employers and other agencies (FEU 1992g). Within colleges staff have been accustomed to work in course teams. They are now working in course curriculum development teams, some of which cross traditional departmental boundaries. Individually they may be contributing elements or modules to courses and individual programmes, for which they have been a member of the planning team, rather than being entirely responsible for a discrete course.

Recent studies have stressed the importance of knowing how students learn and of encouraging active and cooperative learning. A study by Hazel Francis (FEU 1990b) suggests that criteria for the quality of learning should include the need for learners to reflect on what they have learned to demonstrate how a learning task is tackled, and to explain their chosen way of doing a task. A staff development programme to develop observation skills and to understand student learning resulted from the study. It is clear that the lecturer in further education should change from being a didactic purveyor of information and skills to become an effective manager of learning, if the best results are to be obtained.

A curriculum approach

Underling these changes is a move from a traditional curriculum model to a learner-led model. This move is also associated with the wish to develop competences rather than theoretical knowledge. The traditional model, illustrated by Model A, is based on the delivery of a course of a finite length where theory and practice are clearly separated.

Skills and knowledge are not credited as they are acquired but tested by formal examination at the end of the course which the student either passes or fails. Individuals, selected for courses, are put through the same programmes whether they need them or not. There is no recognition of prior learning or of different rates and styles of learning. Student learning is rarely managed and information is delivered didactically in standard forms. The separation of theory from practice leads to outcomes where competence is less important than knowledge.

The learner-led model, Model B, builds on prior learning and envisages a programme in which the competences to be developed are agreed with both sponsors and students. Assessment, diagnosis and the accreditation of prior learning lead to the development of an individual study programme.

This model requires a change in teaching skills from imparting knowledge to more emphasis on assessment, curriculum design, managing student learning and developing competences.

Model B bases education and training on an assessment of individual competences, setting them against the competences required for a qualification or level of performance. An individual programme is planned and its effectiveness is judged on individual performance.

There is conflict between the two models when the learning process is not understood. Government policies, for example, are directed towards developing competences, but educational establishments are expected to produce competences through didactic instruction.

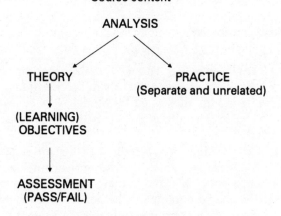

MODEL A
ACTIVITY/PERFORMANCE

Course content

ANALYSIS

THEORY

PRACTICE
(Separate and unrelated)

(LEARNING)
OBJECTIVES

ASSESSMENT
(PASS/FAIL)

Figure 5.1 The traditional curriculum model

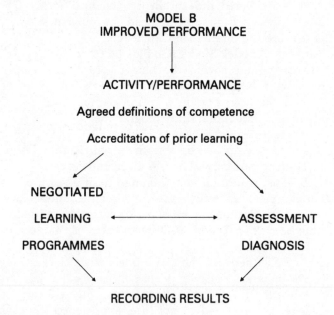

MODEL B
IMPROVED PERFORMANCE

ACTIVITY/PERFORMANCE

Agreed definitions of competence

Accreditation of prior learning

NEGOTIATED

LEARNING ⟷ ASSESSMENT

PROGRAMMES   DIAGNOSIS

RECORDING RESULTS

Figure 5.2 The learner-led model
(These models were outlined by Geoff Staunton of the FEU during a
series of seminars held at the University of London Institute of
Education in 1991/92.)

Curriculum development

The Further Education Unit (FEU) has been very active in curriculum development, and Model B is one suggested outcome of its work. The wider range of students admitted to colleges, the need to provide access to traditional courses, and the changing pattern of qualifications developing through NVQs and GNVQs, have all led to greater attention to learner-led curriculum development (FEU 1989k).

It has been stimulated, in many instances, by the introduction of work-related courses. The students recruited to these courses include those whose experiences of school has been unsatisfactory and whose achievements are often limited. For them the curriculum and its delivery had to be modified both to provide access and to have outcomes which were measurable and acceptable to the sponsors of training.

The introduction of students with disabilities and learning difficulties also drew attention to curriculum development and in particular to the management of individual learning.

The Further Education Staff College (FESC) and the FEU stimulated research, development and guidance which drew the attention of colleges to curriculum planning and development and to effective practices appropriate for all areas of work. Outreach work, collaboration with employers and other agencies and curriculum development have often gone hand in hand (FEU 1989l). Particular emphasis has been placed on the identification and development of core skills, common to a range of areas of study and employment (FEU 1992h). The skills of individual programming and learning management are becoming more important in a learner-led model. These skills, evident in effective work with students with disabilities and learning difficulties, have a much wider application within colleges.

STAFFING AND STAFF DEVELOPMENT

The adequate preparation of all staff is an integral element in managing change and in the implementation of new procedures and practices. Teaching qualifications for further education have not been mandatory and the preparation of staff to work in further education has not always had a high priority. Although preparation existed in a number of specialist centres, professional or technical competence in a particular field was, and still is, a prime requirement (FEU 1992i).

Where students are motivated learners with adequate achievements, and professional and technical courses were unchanging,
problems were limited. However, once a wider student population was being recruited, including reluctant learners and those
with limited learning skills, more attention to teaching and
learning strategies became necessary.

The use of part-time teacher education courses provided by the
City and Guilds Institute and the Royal Society of Arts has
increased. Outreach work by those colleges providing further
education teacher training also made a significant contribution. In-
service education training had a higher profile, stimulated by DES
funding of priority areas of work through a centrally held budget.

Staff preparation to implement change has been receiving a
higher priority. The FESC has provided stimulation in some areas
and colleges have become much more active in developing their
own in- service education programmes (FESC 1990). The FEU has
also developed a wide range of appropriate curriculum materials
for in-service education. Among priorities in recent years have
been information technology and management education. Most
colleges now have a staff development officer with responsibilities
for in-service training.

A particular feature of staffing in recent years has been the
recruitment to colleges of professional non-teaching staff of all
kinds. The emphasis on marketing, for example, has resulted in
specialists in the field being recruited. Increasing independence
will cause more finance and accountancy staff to be recruited. But
the greatest increase has been to support a wide range of different
staff. Not only have the numbers of technicians been increasing
but the complexity of admission procedures, curriculum development, the range of examination systems and requirements,
fund-raising and marketing has necessitated an increase in the
number of administrative support staff.

Staff development has not been confined to teaching staff.
Non-teaching administrative and technical staff have also
required increased training opportunities. These needs were
neglected and had no place in DES funding priorities. They are
now being considered by colleges as part of their staff
development programme (FEU 1987g).

RESPONSIVENESS

Even prior to recent legislation, colleges have been responsive to changing circumstances and demands, as this chapter illustrated. If there is any reluctance to react to more recent pressures it is because there has been underfunding and too much change to absorb into the system. The following chapter will look at other responses in the management and organisation of colleges.

Chapter 6

The college response – current structures

The funding of colleges of further education will be determined by the Further Education Funding Council (FEFC) from April 1993. Training and Education Councils (TECs) will continue to fund their work as Approved Training Organisations. Where colleges retain responsibilities for adult education this will continue to be funded by local education authorities (LEAs). It may be helpful to understand the administrative and organisational structures in place at the beginning of the 1990s. This chapter summarises the background of recent change against which new legislation is being implemented and new developments are taking place.

THE TRADITIONAL PATTERN

The traditional pattern of further education was based on the delivery of discrete vocational courses grouped in departments. A senior team, the principal and vice-principals supported by heads of department, was usually responsible for the management of the college. Each area of work within a department was managed by a course tutor responsible for groups of students enrolled on a particular course.

Colleges have been encouraged to become more businesslike and to involve themselves in direct negotiation with employers and agencies. Full-cost and sponsored courses were introduced. Marketing and income generation by departments became increasingly important. This has also influenced college organisation and internal resource allocation arrangements. FEFC and TEC priorities are also influencing college business and development plans.

ADULT EDUCATION

Adult education, originally a separate service, has been made the responsibility of colleges by some LEAs. Where this is the case, adult education departments provide a complex mixture of vocational and non-vocational work throughout daylight and evening hours. Adult education has not remained non-vocational. It has taken a number of initiatives, all of which increase employability and personal autonomy, and which include:

- adult literacy programmes;
- redundancy and retirement education programmes (FEU 1992i);
- programmes which prepare individuals who have been in long-stay institutions to live and work in the community (FEU 1989n; FEU 1989o; FEU 1989p).

The work of the Adult Literacy and Basic Studies Unit (ALBSU) has been particularly effective in developing appropriate provision within the adult education service for those who wish to improve their educational achievements. Similarly, the Open College has provided a form of vocational preparation through its distance-learning arrangements.

Personal motivation to enhance educational achievements is not always associated with vocational preparation in the first instance. Many adults, particularly women returning to work, look to non-vocational provision as a testing ground for their learning potential and their vocational aspirations. The simple division between vocational work in colleges and non-vocational education in adult institutes no longer holds good – if indeed it ever existed.

Recent government policy has tended to characterise adult education as leisure provision. Funding has been reduced, and with very few exceptions the long-term objective has been a self-financed service. New legislation distinguishes between activities with a vocational objective and all other adult education. Schedule 2 of the Further and Higher Education Act (1992) sets out activities to be considered vocational and thus eligible for FEFC funding.

THE YOUTH SERVICE

The youth service has traditionally been associated with the education service and, in some areas, has worked closely with schools and colleges. Its programme has always included classes or study opportunities of different kinds. More recently, some youth services have moved out of the education service and been grouped with local authority leisure services. However, the service has retained an educative function and further education continues to make a contribution to it.

NEW PATTERNS OF ORGANISATION

The new demands made on colleges have led to the traditional pattern of departments and courses being broken up and new forms of organisation and management developed. Particular factors leading to reorganisation include:

- the increase in the variety of vocational and professional qualifications;
- the development of National Vocational Qualifications (NVQs) (FEU 1989g);
- an increase in demand for shorter updating courses;
- the recognition that the wider range of provision being made has many common elements;
- the accreditation of prior learning (FEU 1992b);
- the development of individual learning programmes.

New flexible patterns of delivery are beginning to emerge. In some colleges modules are being grouped according to curriculum areas, whereas others continue to group courses by vocational areas (FEU 1989r). The recognition that many courses have similar elements, or require similar subject or technological inputs, has resulted in some colleges:

- moving away from a rigid course structure to a modular approach (FEU) 1989q);
- developing staff teams responsible for areas of work or areas of the curriculum (FEU 1990h; FEU 1990i);
- enabling individuals to negotiate their own study programme from an array of modules (FEU 1990j);
- placing increasing emphasis on cross-college provision of all kinds.

The traditional provision of libraries, canteens and student common rooms has been supplemented with a range of other cross-college facilities and services. Libraries have transformed themselves into multi-media resource centres. Other innovations include college information technology services, open learning centres and subject and basic skills workshops (FEU 1987e; FEU 1988k).

Similar changes are taking place in the development of support services for students. Admission procedures are being revised and becoming more systematic. They attempt to determine student needs as well as college requirements (FEU 1989s; FEU 1991d). Careers guidance is becoming an integral part of admission and guidance services. Student counselling, guidance and tutoring services are being expanded and developed, and in some colleges students are now guaranteed specific counselling and tutoring time as part of an entitlement.

Changes in organisation and management resulted in demands for a better college data-base to assist planning. Information gathering and improved communication within colleges were emphasised. Increasing participation rates and expanding the work of the college required attention to marketing. Staff time had to be found for this activity and college organisation had to be modified to respond to the educational needs which arose as a result of marketing.

FUNDING

The traditional entitlement to education up to the age of eighteen-plus has, until recently, been funded through the DES and LEAs. In the past fewer than 50 per cent of school leavers entered colleges. Competing claims from school sixth forms, sixth form colleges and tertiary colleges have meant rival claims for limited resources. In the recent past funding has been diversified. Instead of the vast majority of funds being channelled through the LEAs, the government has been providing specific funding through different departments and agencies. The two main sources of such funding have been the DES and the Department of Employment.

The DES has been supporting access courses for minority groups and funding the Technical Vocational Education Initiative (TVEI) jointly with the Department of Employment. It has also funded staff training in specific areas and more recently governor training. The Department of Employment, working through the Training Agency and subsequently through TECs, has financed youth training and employment training schemes which have varied from year to year. Some health and social service funding has supported developments in community care.

CURRICULUM DEVELOPMENT

At the heart of all the changes taking place in further education is increased attention to curriculum development. The simple acceptance of curricula set down by others has been questioned. The Further Education Unit (FEU) set up with responsibilities for curriculum development, has had a major impact on curricula and methodology in colleges, as the Bibliography shows (FEU 1987f).

A series of very successful publications promoted discussion of the nature, relevance and quality of further education. Colleges are now expected to become more active in this field. One feature to emerge has been the development of modular courses. Modules in different curricular areas were seen as one answer to common elements in different vocational qualifications and to the accreditation of prior learning. Another factor in creating change was the development and introduction of NVQs and General National Vocational Qualifications (GNVQs). The aim is to bring all vocational qualifications within the same framework of four levels of vocational competence. Each NVQ and GNVQ is to be composed of a number of units of competence.

The government is attempting to create a common currency for further education while at the same time encouraging colleges to be active in the development of the means by which agreed curricula are delivered to the very varied groups of students (FEU 1989h). The curriculum for less academic and less successful learners received particular attention as new groups of unemployed young people were recruited to Training Agency-sponsored programmes.

For many such young people the recognition of their progress is vital. Thus it is important to note the different approaches being taken in Scotland and England (FEU 1987; FEU 1989). In Scotland the ScotBec scheme allows modules to be accredited as they are achieved, and an NVQ can be accredited as a result of the accumulation of modules. In England, on the other hand, all modules have to be completed successfully before an NVQ can be awarded. A pass/fail system in England does not recognise partial achievement, and if an individual completes all modules except one, he or she receives no credit at all for successful learning. This approach is not likely to attract or sustain the efforts of reluctant learners or improve their motivation.

CROSS-COLLEGE FACILITIES AND SERVICES

In addition to the quality of common spaces and common social areas there are certain procedures, facilities and services to which all students should have access. The quality of cross-college facilities and services are aspects of college provision which should form part of the entitlement of every student attending the college. Colleges are developing this kind of provision at varying rates, some being well on the way and others just starting.

The quality of cross-college facilities and services, and quality of access to them, is an expression of the college ethos and values experienced daily by staff and students. The descriptions which follow represent a general level of development from which future planning should start. Such facilities and services can be grouped as follows:

1 *Procedures*

- for recruitment and admission;
- for recording and discussing progress;
- for assessing and examining competence;
- for the regulation of staff and student behaviour.

2 *Facilities for learning*

- libraries and multi-media centres;
- information technology support;
- audio-visual aids;
- open learning centres;
- learning support centres.

3 *Personal support services,* including:

- careers guidance;
- personal counselling;
- individual tutoring;
- health and welfare services.

These facilities and services should be available to all students regardless of the way their studies are financed. A major area of debate within colleges has been whether some of them should be provided by staff running courses, by departments or in the form of cross-college provision.

The fourth area, in which facilities and services are developing rapidly, is less directly concerned with students. It concerns the administration of the college and support services for teaching staff.

4 *Administrative services* concerned with:

- a college data-base;
- estate management;
- financial management and resource allocation;
- personnel management;
- secretarial support;
- arrangements for examinations.

Procedures for recruitment and admission have been becoming more sensitive. Marketing has resulted in direct approaches to target groups of potential students. Information about the college programme has been prepared in a more user-friendly way and where necessary in more than one language. Admission procedures have included a diagnostic element to identify possible learning difficulties and needs for support.

Once admitted, procedures to review student progress have become more sensitive and the assessment of competence more practical and relevant to future employment. The ways in which staff and students are expected to conduct themselves in college have been negotiated and codified so that criteria and standards are more explicit and the management of behaviour facilitated.

Facilities for learning have been extended and improved in a number of ways. Libraries have been changing from traditional bases for lending books and reading for reference to multi-media resource centres where information in all forms, delivered by a variety of technologies, is available for teaching and learning (FEU 1989t).

Open learning centres, sometimes associated with the media centres, are being created to provide adults with tailor-made learning packages to improve their learning skills and to enhance their education and vocational proficiency. As a base for distance learning such centres are performing a useful role in extending education to people who cannot attend colleges regularly.

A more recent development has been the setting up of learning support services. These services have developed to meet three main needs:

- the widening range of achievement levels of students admitted to colleges;
- the number of individuals who need their study skills developed or refurbished;
- the admission of students with basic literacy and numeracy needs.

Finally, the increase in provision for students with disabilities and learning difficulties has brought the need to support the learning of individuals on a variety of college programmes. The common response to all these needs has been to set up a centre to which individuals can come for learning support of all kinds and from which staff provide advice and assistance to staff and students elsewhere in the college.

Common services for students have also improved in scope and quality. Personal counselling and careers guidance have assumed greater importance with the extended range of choices available to individuals. The introduction of training credits for young people will increase the need for effective personal guidance services (DE 1990).

An FEU study sees guidance as being offered in three main forms, namely, educational, vocational and personal guidance. It should help individuals to:

- assess their potential;
- identify appropriate opportunities and choose realistic goals;
- increase their awareness of themselves and others;
- become progressively responsible for their own lives.

It concludes that an adequate college guidance service will become increasingly important to the delivery of effective further education (FEU 1987c; FEU 1988l; FEU 1990c).

Less confident learners also respond well to regular tutoring and these services are becoming more common. Many students are faced with social and economic difficulties. Colleges have been developing appropriate personal services to help them. Where such services are not available the learning of some individuals may be seriously affected.

Administrative services The importance of effective administrative services has been recognised. Colleges are dealing with an increasing number of agencies, of funding arrangements and of examining bodies. The introduction of new courses and qualifications and of a wider range of regulations and procedures, together with greater complexity of college organisation, demand considerable administrative skill. A free and effective flow of information and a good communication system are essential.

Administrative and technical support services have been growing and specially qualified staff recruited to meet these demands. The introduction of professionals with accounting and marketing skills has already been mentioned. As well as contributing to policy development these professionals are now forming an important element in the administration of colleges.

From 1993 colleges will be responsible for their budgets, the management of their property, the conditions and terms of service of employees and the legality of all their actions. These increased responsibilities will also entail the employment of appropriately trained staff and, if necessary, the purchasing of external advice and auditing services.

ENTITLEMENT

Mention has already been made of the provision to which clients and students of the college are to be entitled (FEU 1989r). Individual entitlement is part of a growing trend to receive value for money and to establish standards of quality in further and continuing education. The Training Agency and employers wanted clear and defined outcomes for work-related training.

Although attention to value for money has come from sponsors of training, the greater numbers of mature adults now entering colleges have their own higher expectations and pressure for better facilities and services. The central idea of entitlement is that colleges set out:

- what they can offer to all students and how they offer it;
- what students can expect in terms of facilities, the delivery of education programmes and the competence of staff.

As a result students are entitled to expect:

- a curriculum with planned progression in knowledge and competences;
- defined objectives and criteria for successful achievement;

- appropriate levels of staff competence, tutoring and personal support;
- appropriate levels of accommodation, materials and equipment and facilities.

This chapter summarises changes which have taken place in the recent past. In order not to confuse present activity with future development, detailed discussion of many elements has been avoided. As we move from the here-and-now to the immediate future, aspects of college provision and work that are vital to the healthy development of colleges will be discussed in more detail.

Part II

Developing further education

Chapter 7

The parameters

Previous chapters have outlined the changes that have been taking place in the 1980s and major issues being addressed at the beginning of the 1990s. The final chapters look towards the future. The intention of new legislation is to create a further education and training market within which:

- schools, sixth form colleges, further education colleges and training agencies compete for the education and training of the sixteen to nineteen age group;
- further education colleges, adult education institutes and agencies compete to satisfy adult education and training needs.

Educational funding for the sixteen to nineteen age range will now come from two sources:

- the Department for Education (DFE) or local education authorities (LEAs) for sixth forms in secondary schools;
- the Further Education Funding Council (FEFC) for sixth form, tertiary and further education colleges.

The Department of Employment's contribution to vocational preparation will primarily be made through Training and Enterprise Councils (TECs) who are now responsible for youth and employment training. The government also intends that further funding should come from employers who are expected to contribute directly towards the upgrading of the skills of their employees.

Training Credits are being introduced and a first and second series of pilot studies have been carried out. These credits are entitlements to training which are intended to give young people choice in the place, timing and content of a training programme. However, they may be largely channelled through employers and approved training organisations (ATOs) of which the further education college may be one. The FEFC is studying an extension of the training credit scheme which it might finance as one funding option.

The aims of legislation for further and continuing education are compatible with the government's wish to introduce competition and choice in a pursuit of higher standards. It is less certain whether the mechanisms for achieving these objectives will be effective and whether financial arrangements are appropriate. As in other policy areas, the government's approach is to seek an increase in further education opportunities within limited budgets. More for less is how the field views this aspiration.

A significant number of TECs are seeking greater control over vocational education within the work-related non-advanced further education framework. It remains to be seen whether the objectives of TECs and the FEFC are compatible and realistic and whether separate funding and competition for students will create planning difficulties for schools and colleges. The overt and implied value systems of those providing finance and those providing education and training will be significant.

SCHEDULE 2

A distinction between vocational and non-vocational education has been made in the Further and Higher Education Act (1992). It has been expressed in terms of the courses which will be considered to be further education. It is important to look at the definitions set out in Schedule 2, which states that the descriptions of further education are as follows:

a) a course which prepares students to obtain a vocational qualification which is, or falls within a class, for the time being approved for the purposes of this sub-paragraph by the Secretary of State;

b) a course which prepares students to qualify for:
   i) the General Certificate of Secondary Education, or
   ii) the General Certificate of Education at Advanced Level or Advanced Supplementary Level (including Special Papers);

c) a course for the time being approved for the purposes of this sub-paragraph by the Secretary of State which prepares students for entry to a course of higher education;

d) a course which prepares students for entry to another course falling within paragraphs a) to c) above;

e) a course for basic literacy in English;
f) a course to improve the knowledge of English for those for whom English is not the language spoken at home;
g) a course to teach the basic principles of mathematics;
h) in relation to Wales, a course for proficiency or literacy in Welsh;
j) a course to teach independent living and communication skills to persons having learning difficulties which prepare them for entry into another course falling within paragraphs d) to h) above.

These definitions leave a great deal of latitude to the Secretary of State. The relative contributions of colleges and an adult education service have yet to be made clear.

If adult education is recognised as the continuing education which many people of all ages seek, it can play an important part in enhancing the employability and educational level of a wide range of adults of all ages. If it is delegated to a marginal leisure status, many of the aspirations of the new policies may be unfulfilled.

Although the youth service is likely to have a more peripheral relationship to colleges of further education, it is important that colleges maintain an educational presence in youth facilities. These provide a less formal setting within which to motivate the reluctant learner. Outreach work may overcome the disenchantment with education resulting from being unsuccessful and undervalued in school.

The interpretation of Schedule 2 will be crucial. Different funding agencies will have different priorities, and inconsistencies may occur. It is important for colleges to develop a rationale for their Schedule 2 contribution (See Figure 7.1).

MAJOR OBJECTIVES

Within this framework of change three main objectives for the education and training system have been identified. Colleges of further and continuing education are expected to:

- increase participation;
- improve standards;
- prepare young people and adults for an effective working life.

These aims are interrelated and their achievement will be influenced by the value systems of colleges and the inclusiveness of their policies. Governors and senior management teams will be expected to administer colleges on sound commercial lines and achieve increased participation and improved quality.

INDEPENDENCE AND VALUES

It is worth summarising some of the issues already discussed as a context for future developments. These include values, inclusiveness and potential. All businesses and organisations have value systems which have implications for customers. Similarly further education institutions convey implicit and explicit values, often differently perceived by learners and teachers. Colleges, with other trainers and TECs, will become responsible for the ethics of post-school education and training. To do this, governors and senior managers will need to consider the following questions:

- What is the purpose of the college?
- Who are the customers?
- What values are explicit or implicit in the college development plans and other publications?
- Do policies and practices demonstrate these values in practice?
- What conceptual framework informs college policies and practices?

A conceptual framework and value system on which to base a development plan is essential if pressures from commerce, industry, the local community and a variety of other groups are to be harnessed within a coherent set of priorities.

There has been a tradition of staff and students being valued according to the academic or technical level of work they do. More recently an opposite trend has been evident in some colleges, namely, to accord equal value to all students. An effective equal opportunities policy, for example, values the potential of all individuals and allocates resources to redress disadvantages.

Economic pressures, which encourage colleges to value students according to the resources they contribute, will make it difficult to sustain an equal opportunities policy unless it is recognised that higher unit costs are involved when students are hard to educate. A statement of college policies may be an important beginning, but sponsors and students soon become aware of an implicit value system. Questions which are raised include:

- Are some students valued more highly than others because of the resources they generate?
- Do all students have an equal entitlement to the same quality of instruction, materials and facilities?

As with the previous questions, the answers reflect a value system conveyed by policies, practices and the marketing strategy of the college.

PURCHASERS, PROVIDERS AND STUDENTS

'Purchasers', 'providers', 'clients' and 'customers' are all words entering the further education field from business management. The one word which remains the clear prerogative of education is 'student' and even here this is often thought to be an inadequate term to describe adult learners. The independence of colleges and the values they represent are now increasingly influenced by the relationships between purchasers and providers of education and training.

Colleges must be clear about their relative responsibilities to those who pay and those who learn. Who are the clients/ customers? Are they students or sponsors of education and training? Colleges will have to prepare and make known their strategic and business plans as part of their submissions to the FEFC. These submissions will represent the interface between the Council's values and those of the college. The effective college with a coherent strategy will probably have more scope for manoeuvre than one whose submissions are fragmented and piecemeal.

INCLUSIVENESS AND POTENTIAL

A college's approach to inclusiveness and student potential will be set in its ethical framework. Both are related to outcomes like academic standards and technical competence as well as to the ways in which they are achieved. Exclusiveness does not always result in high standards, or inclusiveness in lower ones. Although the level from which you start may be significant, it is the progress made by students which is a major indicator of quality. It is important to recognise and measure progress, the value-added aspect of education.

A philosophy of inclusiveness assumes that, within staffing and resource limits, colleges will attempt to provide for the educational needs of as wide a cross-section of the local adult population as possible. As well as being responsive to TEC priorities and to the needs of commerce and industry, they will also seek to increase participation from all sections of the community. Colleges may also seek to recruit students from the wider community of Europe and elsewhere in the world.

Another important contribution of colleges is the further education and training of professionals in local authority and public services and the personal and skill-development needs of adults, of all levels of ability and aptitude, in different phases of their lives.

Both positive and negative student potential has to be considered. Colleges are well used to attempting to recruit students with more and more potential as they strive to achieve higher status. This trend is currently being confirmed by the need for higher education institutions to franchise colleges of further education to develop first-year degree work.

Because the social and economic costs of potentially difficult to educate and train students do not fall on the education system, there is less enthusiasm for recruiting students whose potential may be hard to realise. The long-term costs of unemployment, of a lifetime on benefits and pensions, and of being undervalued in the community are far greater than the cost of appropriate education and training. Colleges which are sensitive to these issues will also be concerned to be inclusive.

If further education is narrowly conceived, every new additional group is seen as creating precedents and as such potentially disruptive of the status quo. Inclusiveness is made much harder to achieve if admission to programmes is based on levels of achievement which exclude large sectors of the community and if the learner is required to produce evidence of achievements not easy for some individuals and groups to acquire. The wider the population basis on which the college programme is initially planned, the easier it will be to accommodate variations in individual demands, learning styles and rates of learning. This will be because the college takes a broad approach to the assessment of prior learning and has in place flexible systems for managing and supporting learning.

COLLEGES ARE DYNAMIC ORGANISATIONS

Colleges move through phases of growth, decline and development as staff and student populations change. They are composed of groups of individuals who may or may not have common purposes and who have the potential to cope with or defend against change. The ability of the college to respond to changed circumstances, to be flexible and to anticipate future demands are some indicators of its effectiveness. Its inclusive approach to admissions and the way resources are used and to the dynamic development of staff and student potential are other important indicators.

Colleges need to look ahead to predict and anticipate trends and future demands. This too is part of a dynamic approach to planned growth or planned retrenchment and effective development programmes. You may be on the right lines but if you stand still you will be run over by progress.

INCREASED PARTICIPATION

Within its value system a college will attempt to achieve the three major objectives set out earlier. The first and most important objective, increased participation, implies a better-educated population. The second and third objectives, improved standards and adequate preparation for an adult working life, are vital for industrial and commercial competitiveness. Continued education and the upgrading of skills make an essential contribution to such competitiveness and are an integral part of life-long learning.

Increased participation requires colleges to be sensitive to the educational and training needs of commerce, industry, public services and the adult population in the community they serve. A 'needs analysis' is an essential prerequisite to the development of a marketing strategy.

The college must be proactive, taking steps to identify educational and training needs. Marketing, informed by local demands, together with accurate information about what is on offer, should attract students. Sensitive counselling, guidance and admission procedures should then encourage students to enrol and welcome them to the college. The college must do more than merely react to demands.

A number of actions will need to be taken if there is to be sufficient data to complete a needs analysis. It will be necessary for the college to:

- conduct an audit of its resources (FEU 1989k);
- carry out a detailed survey of other provision in the area;
- know the funding priorities of agencies, particularly those of local TECs.

The difference between the wants and needs of potential sponsors/clients and students should also be analysed so that it becomes possible to:

- look at the match between education and training needs in the area served by the college, and the current student population, taking into account other provision in the area;
- study the match between education and training demands the college might meet, and the available resources;
- determine and agree college priorities;
- produce a college development plan to implement them.

A marketing strategy and approach should not only be evident in all contacts with local commerce, industry and other groups in the community but should also permeate all areas of college work (FEU/FESC 1985). As well as setting out to attract a wider range of students (FEU 1989f), the strategy should also include an effective equal opportunities policy.

Potential students may include people not previously well catered for, for example, young people who have been less successful in school, under-represented adult groups, women returners and young people and adults with disabilities and learning difficulties. Adults with literacy and numeracy needs, though often seen as a separate group, also fall broadly within the general population from whom increased participation is to be encouraged. All these potential students may require special arrangements for their access to education and learning support throughout their time in college.

Measures to attract the disenchanted and reluctant learner should be part of a strategy to attract a wider group of students (FEU 1991e). Outreach work and a close association with community groups may also play a part. However, financial arrangements may not provide any inducement to recruit this group, and financial incentives to both colleges and students may be necessary.

It is important that colleges take a long-term view of learning and that staff are aware of the need to pay attention to progression. Guidance and counselling should encourage students to continue to develop their knowledge and skills by different means, at different times and in different ways over a period of time. Participation is increased when students are encouraged to consider the next steps they might take, and staff build progression into their individual programmes.

Increased participation should be a concern of the whole college. All departments should make their programmes accessible to the widest possible range of students and increase participation through supporting the learning of less confident students. Increased participation is not simply a matter of providing for more separate specialist groups.

IMPROVED STANDARDS

To increase participation it is necessary to identify potential students and develop profiles of their educational and training needs. But unless this is accompanied by the provision of appropriate education of high quality, potential students may not be recruited. Thus increased participation and quality are closely linked.

Standards of education and training are assessed from different points of view. For example, by:

- college staff;
- students;
- clients and sponsors;
- external evaluators.

Standards are assessed in a quantitative and a qualitative manner:

- Quantitative standards are expressed in terms of the number of people who achieve a level of competence and are judged simply by outcomes.
- Qualitative standards are set by the way people achieve and demonstrate a level of competence and also take into account the processes by which outcomes are achieved.

Attention to the processes by which competences are achieved is what distinguishes an educational approach from that of training. Education should be concerned with the continued development of performance. Minimum performance is not enough. For example, people can pass driving tests and remain relatively unskilled; others continue to develop into very competent drivers.

It is vitally important to demonstrate competences at the end of all programmes of education and training.

The perspective from which an aspect of education and training is assessed may influence the judgement of standards by internal and external assessors.

- It may be important to know whether the assessor knows only a single college or whether he or she knows the work of many colleges in different parts of the country.
- Sponsors of training may have a different perspective from college managers which, in turn, may be different to that of students.

In practice, the perspective of the assessor may be crucial. If the student does not agree with the views of the sponsor or college management about the quality of the setting or the education and training provided, effective learning is unlikely to take place.

Government initiatives are aimed at questioning the academic and vocational hierarchy which influences the choices of young people and their parents, and at narrowing the gap between academic and technical proficiency. Educational standards will now be embodied in a system of qualifications of two kinds. National Vocational Qualifications (NVQs) and General National Vocational Qualifications (GNVQs). NVQs will be outcome-related and set agreed levels of competence in vocational areas. GNVQs, on the other hand, are aimed at developing achievements and competences of more general application in a number of fields of employment and will also be concerned with processes. A conflict between the two approaches seems inevitable. It epitomises the unresolved question of the relative values of education and training.

All the main providers of funds to colleges are seeking the introduction of quality assurance into the further education and training system. The FEFC is required to have a quality-assurance committee. At present, individual and departmental standards within colleges are patchy and inconsistent.

Entitlement and standards

The achievement of higher standards should not be divorced from student entitlement. College standards are not only an expression of its competence and effectiveness but also an indication of what students who attend it are entitled to expect.

Standards set by institutions and accreditation bodies can be assessed in terms of:

- the quality of the facilities, equipment and curricula a college provides for all students;
- the quality of the delivery of learning opportunities to all students;
- what the institution expects of students during their programmes;
- the outcomes achieved by students.

Individual entitlement, implicit in the achievement of standards, requires that the college provides the courses, modules, facilities or services described in its prospectus and that what is provided is of a reasonable and consistent standard.

Entitlement, determined by individual colleges, will vary. It can be broken down into constituent parts. For example, an environmental entitlement might include well-appointed public spaces, hygienic toilet and washing facilities and premises with high health and safety standards. A curriculum entitlement might include well-prepared learning materials, appropriate equipment and a clear statement of curriculum intentions and objectives. Finally, a learning support entitlement might include the availability of library and multi-media resources, open learning opportunities and arrangements to foster and improve learning skills.

Institutions will have implicit or explicit notions of entitlement and of standards. It is equally important that colleges describe the ways in which standards are determined and how their achievement is to be assessed. A market approach demands that colleges make their standards and student entitlements explicit.

CONDITIONS FOR LEARNING

There are a number of important aspects of learning to be considered at this point. They include the accreditation of prior learning, interactive learning, differentiated learning and open learning. Staff in colleges are currently concerned with developing all of them.

Accrediting prior learning   In order to make effective use of teacher and learner time it is important that substantive prior learning is recognised and used as a starting-point for the development of individual programmes. There are two aspects to accreditation, namely, the level and proficiency of learning or study skills and competences in a subject or skill area.

A number of practical problems are now being tackled. They include:

- the varying length of programmes;
- their funding when prior learning is accredited;
- the development of college structures to encompass accreditation;
- the implications of accreditation for the management of differentiated learning.

Interactive learning   Further education has traditionally placed reliance on courses in which groups of individuals follow the same curriculum over the same period of time. They have been taught as a group, starting from the same base-line. Interactive learning and group work have tended to be at best patchy and often unplanned spin-offs from practical work. More recently, the value of different modes and rates of learning has been appreciated.

Most young people and adults learn from each other, and a well-motivated group can facilitate the learning of its individual members. There should be planned occasions for working with others in most individual programmes or courses of study. All learners are stimulated by positive group activities. Many adult learners, particularly those returning to learning and reluctant young learners, need the encouragement of shared success, cooperation and mutual support. The curriculum and its delivery, the settings in which students are taught, and cross-college learning support facilities should encourage the social interaction vital to effective learning.

The recognition of prior learning and the development of individual learning programmes, made possible by a flexible approach to learning and facilitated by technology, should not reduce attention to learning as a social activity.

Differentiated learning   The traditional method of teaching classes the same things at the same pace is slowly being replaced by differentiated learning. This involves the management of learning and relies heavily on a knowledge of students' levels of achievement and rates and styles of learning. Staff with this knowledge plan different objectives and programmes for individuals and small groups within the class.

Open learning   Open learning opportunities also have much to offer adult learners. The work of the National Extension College and its increasing student body is evidence of this. To be successful, an open learning centre needs a wide range of distance-learning material and computer-programmed material. Most important of all are staff sensitive to individual learning needs, skilled in matching materials and needs and experienced in counselling and tutoring.

Planned individual study, group work and open learning opportunities are becoming more common (FESC 1991). Increased participation involves a greater understanding of the learning process in order to provide a broad range of learning opportunities for students, with a wider variety of rates and styles of learning. Individual programmes should include short courses and modules, as well as open learning and individual study. An individual learning programme should not, however, result in solitary learning.

ACCREDITATION

In addition to the recognition of previous individual learning, accreditation validates programmes offered by colleges. A significant factor in increasing standards is the accreditation of courses, modules and qualifications. Accreditation of further education courses was, until recently, undertaken by a variety of agencies and was based on prescribed courses of study over a specified time.

The setting up of the NVQ scheme (FEU 1990a) is an attempt to develop a single system of accreditation in which different levels of competence are agreed with the industries and services for which they are designed. Existing agencies will continue to administer schemes of accreditation but within a national framework.

Progress through a system of NVQs will be recorded on a National Record. The NVQ scheme changes the emphasis from courses to learner-led and negotiated individual programmes which recognise and build on prior learning. Outcomes, with a new emphasis on competence as well as on knowledge, are assessed when the individual can demonstrate appropriate skills and knowledge, not at the end of fixed periods.

COUNCILS AND FUNDING PRIORITIES

Aspirations and values are important for the staff of colleges whose conceptual framework will influence practical issues. The priorities of three major funding bodies, the FEFC, TECs and LEAs, together with those of employers, will influence financing and planning college programmes. The European Community may also have an increasing influence through grants and the harmonisation of qualifications.

FEFC   The primary purpose of the Council is to promote an effective range of education and financing opportunities. Colleges are responsible for planning and delivering programmes funded by the Council. They will be expected to be creative and imaginative in the proposals they make and more and more proficient at formulating them. Although proposals should reflect the education and training needs of the areas from which colleges recruit, the Council will have an overall view of national needs. New funding arrangements may result in a more consistent and systematic distribution of the resources available and greater equity in national standards of provision.

TECs   The Councils are still determining their priorities but they are already making it clear that they have insufficient resources to carry out their programmes. Limited resources are forcing them to go for quick and inexpensive training packages, an approach not likely to increase participation and meet the needs of those who are more expensive and harder to train.

Training Credits   It is far from clear whether individuals will be trusted to use Training Credits or whether their use will be heavily influenced by sponsors of training. The results of pilot schemes are being evaluated. It is already clear that potential employability is influencing their allocation and that this is assessed on past achievements and not on responses to post-school education and training.

Sponsorship   In the past LEAs have been responsible for further and continuing education in a range of institutions including psychiatric hospitals and prisons. Colleges now have an opportunity to act as sponsors for these forms of educational provision. They will be expected to submit bids to the FEFC, in competition with private firms, for undertaking post-sixteen education in a whole range of institutions. The Council's conditions for sponsorship are that:

- a significant proportion of provision is within Schedule 2 of the Further and Higher Education Act (1992);
- colleges have the ability to assume the responsibilities of incorporation;
- there are satisfactory financial prospects;
- there has been full exploration of other funding options;
- there has been consultation with other interested parties;
- the proposal is approved by the governing body where sponsored work is to be carried out.

MAJOR INFLUENCES ON FURTHER EDUCATION

The government wishes to see the FEFC, TEC and commercial and industrial sponsorship having the most influence on college priorities. Such responsibilities as remain to LEAs, particularly in the sixteen to nineteen age range, will be much more difficult to exercise. What is less certain is the extent to which community needs, not necessarily associated with specific funding, will influence the provision made.

While LEAs have been encouraging colleges in their areas to develop a coherent pattern of provision, new funding arrangements will be encouraging competition. Minority group interests have had their place in LEA strategic plans but there is less certainty that individual colleges, in competition with each other, will give such needs adequate priority.

In time the FEFC and TECs may be expected to have their own strategic plans and system of priorities. This framework will be necessary if funding is to be used economically. Developing an effective response to education and training requires time, resources and a framework of medium-term priorities. Staff often have to be retrained to plan new forms of provision and prepare materials and equipment. Further education cannot be planned on the basis of changing annual grant priorities and arrangements.

Incorporation has involved the senior management teams of

colleges in a major reorganisation of college administrative procedures. The strategic thinking of such teams has not always been communicated to middle management and other staff who are often ill informed about the new contexts in which they have to work.

Communication and discussion of college aspirations and plans are urgent necessities after incorporation if staff are to be enabled to make an effective contribution. Values and standards, if not clearly stated at the outset, will be made explicit in funding priorities. Colleges must develop their own value systems if they are to maintain a sense of direction towards agreed objectives. For example, it may be necessary to ration the provision of prestige courses or expensive equipment in order to provide essential services for the general population of students. While it is important that sponsors of education and training should influence further education, only colleges can represent and defend the interests of all students.

In this chapter, concerned with the future development of further education and training, the importance of values and standards has been stressed. Commercial and industrial values have not always been positive for the work-force. Now that there is greater concern to have a well-educated and trained work-force it is vital that colleges have a sound value system. Equal opportunities must exist in practice as well as in mission statements. Students must be recognised as having equal entitlements to standards and quality, whatever the level of their needs or achievements. The implications of these statements for colleges are discussed in the next chapter.

The FEFC is making strenuous efforts to consult widely and develop its priorities and procedures in collaboration with colleges. There is less evidence of this approach being reflected in colleges. But it is to be hoped that the next decade will see more open discussion about the development of further education and training as a coherent and equitable system available to all.

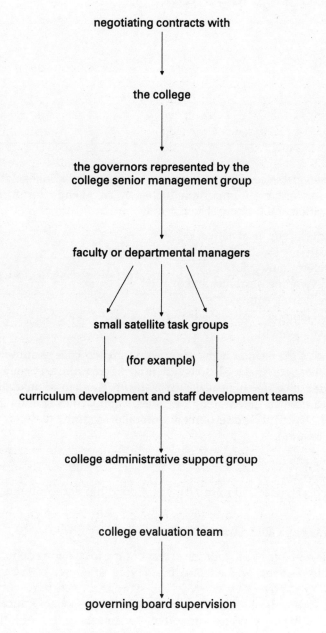

Figure 7.1 Developing a rationale

Chapter 8

A college agenda

Whatever the conceptual framework adopted by a college, there are a number of important items on an agenda for further education and training. They include:

- developing local networks;
- fostering local collaboration or competition;
- determining priorities;
- developing flexibility and quality;
- delivering equity;
- developing cost-effectiveness and economic resource management.

None of the agenda items are new but greater college autonomy and changes in legislation and funding require that they are tackled in different ways. Two elements need to be taken into account when determining priorities, organisation and management structures and resource allocation procedures.

These are:

- management and resourcing of cross-college facilities and services;
- maintenance and improvement of buildings and equipment.

FLEXIBLE COLLEGES

Colleges have had a tradition of responding to changing demands. In the past this was effected by varying the range of the time-limited courses they offered. The significant feature of current demands is flexible learning opportunities. The Further Education Unit (FEU) has produced important documents on this topic (FEU

1991d), arguing that it is necessary to introduce flexible learning in order to:

- increase access to learning for individuals so that they can realise their potential to contribute to a better trained and qualified work-force;
- remove barriers to learning such as attendance requirements, entry qualifications, individual learning difficulties;
- increase the effectiveness of learning by making it learner-centred, shaped by individual starting-points, prior learning, preferred learning styles and purposes;
- enable people to take responsibility for their own learning within a framework of appropriate support.

Differences between a 'course-based' college and a 'learner-centred' college are set out in terms of marketing and outreach, threshold services, flexible access to learning, flexible access to assessment and accreditation, supported learning and the college infrastructure. The move away from a college organisation into which potential students are expected to fit to one which is flexible enough to respond to a range of individual education and training needs as they arise, demands a number of changes.

The Flexible College (FEU 1991d) gives guidance about making the necessary changes in college structures and procedures. Under each heading characteristics are described and subsequent sections indicate the steps that have to be taken for the transition to a learner-centred college. For example:

- marketing needs to be proactive in schools, employment and adult guidance services, and colleges need access to good labour market intelligence;
- threshold services should provide a welcome in an adult environment, continuous access to guidance and enrolment throughout the year, comprehensive information about the location of appropriate assessment, learning and training opportunities, guidance to clarify individual objectives and the accreditation of prior learning;
- there should be a range of available modes of learning, an individual learning programme based on a modular cur-riculum with clear learning and competence objectives, unit accreditation, roll-on-roll-off access to modules and the provision of learning support;
- there should be flexible access to diagnostic assessment with the

accreditation of prior learning and transferable module and unit credits;

- the infrastructure should increase participation, initiate new models of resource allocation based on units of achievement delivered, deploy staff flexibly, create a wide variety of learning environments and have clear performance indicators for staff and services.

It is essential that the development model for any educational institution pays attention to the process by which results are obtained as well as to the achievement of those results.

QUALITY: RAISING STANDARDS

A second major objective of government policies is to raise the standards of education and training so that the staffing needs of industry and commerce are met and the country has a highly skilled work-force. This search for quality is an area where colleges are learning from industry. A number of models, BS5750 and TQM are two, now in use (FEU 1987a; ETA 1988, FEU/Pick-Up 1988).

While industrial and commercial models may be helpful in the short term, it will be necessary for further education to develop its own methods of quality assurance. Quality standards in further education are essentially concerned with human performance and need to be measured accordingly.

Confusion may arise in the use of the word 'quality'. '*A* quality' of something is not always distinguished from '*the* quality' of the same thing. For example, flexibility may be a quality of elastic, but elastic may be of good or bad quality as a result of its production. In this section the word 'quality' is used to describe the standards achieved in the provision of further education. The two things that colleges are seeking to develop are 'quality control' and 'quality assurance'.

Improving standards involves raising the quality of teaching and learning and improving student performance. *Quality Matters* (FEU 1991) describes models and sets out a number of these important considerations.

The means of improving quality must:

- be flexible;
- involve all teaching and non-teaching staff, harnessing their efforts towards common objectives;

- involve learners, in commenting on experiences of the learning process;
- establish measures of requirements and outcomes so that progress can be proved;
- be based on procedures experienced and accepted by all concerned as reasonable.

Two important aspects of improving quality are:

- *Quality control,* which involves using operational techniques and standard procedures to ensure that products conform to specification. In further education and training this means that the work of students completing curriculum modules or programmes is of an appropriate standard and they demonstrate defined competences;
- *Quality assurance,* which describes the checks and audits which ensure that quality-control procedures are followed and are effective.

Performance indicators of quality were the subject of a study by the FEU (FEU 1991c) and indicators suggested included:

- student/staff ratios;
- unit costs linked to output indicators;
- non-teacher cost per enrolled full-time student;
- space utilisation.

It has already been pointed out that quality can be assessed from different perspectives by colleges, customers/students, clients/ sponsors and external evaluators. Clients or sponsors of training may have a different perspective from the college managers', which may be different from that of students. In practice the perspective of the assessor may be crucial. If the student does not agree with the views of the education and training sponsor or college management about the quality of the setting or the education and training provided, effective learning is unlikely to take place.

It is also important to recognise that quality standards involve staff appraisal procedures. For example, one aspect of staff competence might be the management of learning. Such management can be good, bad or indifferent and it will be necessary to decide what criteria are used to assess the quality of the management of learning.

College managers, therefore, have to do two different things in their search for quality. They have to identify the elements which they consider essential to an appropriate educational offering and also determine the criteria to be used to assure the quality of the element offered. They have to develop a cycle of quality assurance which includes the perspectives of all the participants and sponsors of further education.

DELIVERING EQUITY

Many aspects of delivering equity have already been outlined in a discussion of the inclusive college (see Chapter 7). Many others are implicit in the move from traditional approaches to a learner-led model. Given flexible access to further education and training, what else might be involved in delivering equity within colleges?

Access to all college facilities and services is a first essential. It has been the practice in some colleges to assume that students with disabilities and learning difficulties do not need access to the same facilities as others, or that 'low-level' students do not need up-to-date technology.

Training for the Future (FEU 1990k) outlines another approach based on assignments delivered by interdisciplinary course teams. The concept of key technologies is central to the development of assignments and the equalising of opportunity. However, the main ingredient to delivery equity must be the quality of the curriculum, the equipment and materials necessary for its delivery and the ways in which it is delivered. There should not be a quality hierarchy based on the academic or technical level of students or their work.

COST-EFFECTIVENESS

The incorporation of colleges makes the question of cost-effectiveness a priority. It is closely associated with the management structure of the college and the levels of accountability built into it. The governors will need to agree a business plan for the college and have available a monthly statement of college finances. These are essential if the governors and senior managers are to keep a close eye on financial trends and get early warning of impending problems.

It will be necessary for resource allocation to be related to middle management and course team levels. If departments or faculties are to be middle management units, their financial accountability will be a vital element in cost-effectiveness. Equally important will be a close watch on the cost of the growing administrative and accountancy element in college management.

PLANT AND BUILDINGS

When local education authorities (LEAs) administered colleges they were responsible for new capital investment and the maintenance of buildings and plant. Because their resources were constantly reduced by central government, many colleges were not well maintained (FESC 1986). Although colleges will take up their financial responsibilities without the burden of debt, they will not take over any funds for the maintenance of buildings or the improvement of facilities.

Although the Further Education Funding Council (FEFC) takes over the Department of Further Education (DFE) capital works programme, the way the Council will handle this problem is uncertain (FEFC Circular 92/17). It is unlikely to have sufficient funds to deal with the backlog of necessary work and it will be important to establish clear national priorities for the maintenance and development of buildings and plant.

MANAGING AND RESOURCING CROSS-COLLEGE SERVICES

The funding of these facilities and services is a matter of some concern where financing is exclusively output-related. It seems likely that the introduction of Training Credits and of the accreditation of prior learning will bring some funding for guidance counselling and assessment services in colleges.

It is likely that colleges will be expected to determine their own priorities, and thus the priority given to open learning centres and learning support services may vary from college to college. Priorities may also be influenced by the ways in which education and training programmes are financed. Colleges which give such provision a high priority may fund it from within their total budget by deducting agreed elements, top-slicing allocations to departments, faculties and courses.

COLLABORATION, COMPETITION AND NETWORKS

Competition between colleges in a post-sixteen market place for education and training may be the objective of new legislation. However, colleges may react in other ways. Survival in that market place may depend on collaboration and becoming part of a network.

Except for those with a particular national contribution to make, most colleges will function in a geographical area where there are other colleges and training agencies. In such circumstances cooperative arrangements with neighbouring colleges and joint bids for training initiatives will be possible. Training consortia may be set up with others. Arrangements of this kind may be essential for the stability and continuity of some educational and training options. The FEFC has already issued guidance on mergers and amalgamations (FEFC Circular 92/14).

Other contributions to sustainability include the appointment of members of Training and Enterprise Councils (TECs) to boards of corporations and the building up of a network of potential education and training sponsors and employers. Colleges will have continually to re-establish their credibility with those who fund them and those who accept or employ their ex-students.

A CHECK-LIST

It may be helpful at this point to set out a check-list for the development of colleges. It covers management, buildings and accommodation, marketing and finance, organisation, the curriculum and support services.

Management

The board and management of colleges should check that:

- the board is well informed about the work of the college;
- there are governing board members who are knowledgeable about all aspects of college activities, including work with minority groups;
- there is a senior management team with access to high-quality advice from educational, financial, legal, marketing and management professionals;

- there is a college management structure which facilitates the effective achievement of its objectives by the college.

Buildings and accommodation

The senior management team should have:

- carried out a survey of all college buildings and facilities to see that they are of an appropriate standard for the work or activity for which they are designated;
- ensured that all buildings and facilities are accessible and available to all students;
- produced a programme for maintenance work and the use of accommodation to implement the college development plan.

Marketing and finance

The board and senior management team should have ensured that:

- they has appointed staff with appropriate qualifications and experience in the fields of marketing and financial management;
- a business plan is prepared with the Director of Finance and is updated annually;
- staff responsible for marketing the college are well informed about all potential student needs;
- finance staff are aware of all the means of funding students and familiar with all statutory and voluntary sources of support for them.

Organisation

The board should ensure that the college has an up-to-date and revised:

- three- to five-year strategic plan;
- equal opportunities policy statement

and that there is:

- a flexible range of provision for all students, designed to encompass the wide range of individual variations in style and pace of learning;

- fair and equitable distribution of resources and staff to all aspects of college work;
- weighting for programmes and for support to individuals which acknowledges varying levels of complexity and need;
- an effective system of liaison with schools and other agencies, including employers, for recruitment and entry of students to the college;
- an admission system, with information in appropriate forms, to facilitate applications for places;
- a comprehensive system of guidance, support and counselling available during students' period in college and for their entry into work.

There should also be an appropriate system of evaluation and quality assurance which:

- has clear performance indicators, similar in rigour throughout the college;
- ensures that the education offered to all students is of a high quality.

The curriculum

It is also necessary to check that the curriculum and its modules, units and courses provide:

- a flexible range of learning opportunities from which individuals can develop individual learning programmes;
- access to the same range of curricular opportunities for all students, all students being recognised as having the same curriculum entitlements;
- continuity and progression for the individual.

It is also necessary to ensure that there is:

- an adequate range of teaching and learning areas, equipment and materials to support individual learning programmes throughout the college.

Support systems

A number of important aspects need to be checked during admission procedures. These include:

- appropriate arrangements to ascertain and accredit prior learning;
- the identification of individual learning needs and, where they exist, learning support needs;
- sensitivity to minority group needs;
- sensitivity to individual needs for personal support.

Support systems to sustain effective learning need to be checked to ensure that all students have access to:

- counselling and guidance services;
- tutorial support according to the nature and complexity of individual need;
- health service and psychological service support;
- personal welfare services;
- external statutory and voluntary support services.

These check-lists are not complete and many other items could be listed. What they attempt to do is to show that a college's response to its local community is not simply a matter of being there. A lot of systems have to be put in place before a college can make an effective response to the educational and training needs in the area it sets out to serve. The following chapter will outline one model which reflects a college response to the agenda discussed here.

The FEFC requires colleges to analyse educational needs in the local community and include provision for them in their strategic plans. These plans should also show the provision to be made for students with disabilities and learning difficulties. The FEFC is giving an important lead through its papers and Circulars as to how it sees the future for colleges.

Chapter 9

Implications for college governors and managers

A NEW APPROACH

The 1990s and beyond will create new conditions for further education and training. External conditions will include new funding arrangements and a comparative freedom from control by elected members of local authorities. Internal conditions will include the accreditation of prior learning, open and self-directed learning, and emphasis on individual programmes. All these factors will lead to the introduction of new techniques and learning strategies.

College responses to change have varied from hoping it will never happen, through *ad hoc* responses, to a radical reappraisal of policies, priorities and programmes. As previous chapters have shown, an adequate college response can only develop from a clear conceptual framework for the provision of further education and training. This chapter outlines the essential features of a data-base and a model developed by the Further Education Unit (FEU) which might prove helpful in developing such a conceptual framework.

THE COLLEGE APPROACH

Governors, together with the senior management team, will need to determine an appropriate role for the college in the community it serves. A first step in this process will be to conduct an audit of college facilities and resources (FEU 1989k). Before looking in detail at plans, governors and senior managers, together with external assessors if necessary, should carry out an educational audit to determine:

- quality and cost of existing elements in the college programme;
- extent and quality of existing human and other resources;
- whether resources are adequate to deliver education and training of quality (FEU 1992j);

- what reallocation of resources, or additional resources, are necessary to extend college work and raise quality to the desired standard (FESC 1988, 1991).

At the same time a discussion of education and training needs should take place with all the different potential sponsors and students in the community served by the college. As a result of the audit and consultation a clear sense of purpose and direction for the college should be identified, with a statement of the aims and aspirations to provide a framework for detailed plans (Industry Matters 1988). Continuous interaction should occur as the aspirations of the college are modified in the light of consultation with funding agencies, sponsors and potential students.

A number of important college values and standards will be explicit or implicit in these plans. Identified needs have to be matched against aims for the college and the resources available to it. As a result, governors and senior managers should also be able to answer questions asked earlier which are repeated here because of their importance:

- What is the principal purpose of the college?
- On what conceptual framework is the college's development based?
- What values are explicit or implicit in its policies?
- What should be the main priorities in the college plan?
- What are the short- and long-term objectives of its work?
- How do these objectives relate to the objectives of other further education and training provision in the immediate area?

With the data-base provided by an audit, the answers to these questions should provide a basis on which to develop plans. The preparation of strategic and tactical development plans (FEU 1989u) and a business plan (Richardson 1989) should follow, setting out more detailed objectives and specifying what the college can offer. FEFC Circular 92/18 sets out a procedure for planning with which the suggested model is compatible (Figure 9.4).

A MODEL FOR PLANNING

Before looking at the elements in college plans it may be helpful to consider a model on which to base them. This model was developed in a series of seminars held at the London Institute of Education in 1990–91 and subsequently published as a discussion document *Supporting Learning* (FEU 1992e). The seminars were primarily concerned with the establishment of a framework for meeting the needs of students with disabilities and learning difficulties. However, it became apparent that an effective approach to meeting the needs of these students could not be developed in isolation from the organisation of the college as a whole, and that many of the features of an inclusive approach were equally valid for all students. The brief description which follows draws attention to the model's essential features.

A philosophy of inclusiveness, already outlined, assumes that a college will attempt to provide for as wide a cross-section of educational needs in the local population of young people and adults as is possible within existing staffing and resource limits. The model assumes that college policies are not only directed to an absolute increase in the number of students but are equally committed to increasing the range of students for whom provision of quality is made.

In practice, colleges provide some facilities and services for all students, develop variations in working conditions for major groups of students, and make specific arrangements for minority needs and interests. While it may be true that provision for minority needs tends in practice to be for high-status groups of students, the three aspects of provision are a useful basis on which to plan provision more generally.

The model suggested by the FEU distinguishes three levels of provision:

1) *Core elements.* Facilities and services to which all students receiving the education and training in the college are entitled;
2) *Common necessary variants.* Facilities and services which provide for common variations in course requirements and facilities and reflect the range of opportunities the college can provide;
3) *Specific necessary variants.* Specific facilities and services which support the education and training of particular groups and individuals.

The following diagrams were devised as part of an FEU seminar series, held in association with the Institute of Education, University of London.

The borderline between these three groups of facilities and services, the core, common necessary variants and specific necessary variants, must be flexible. In practice the larger the core,

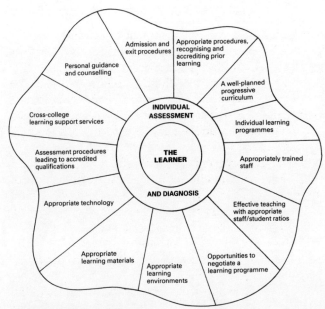

Figure 9.1 Core elements
Source: FEU *Supporting Learning: Part 1 – A Model for Colleges* © FEU

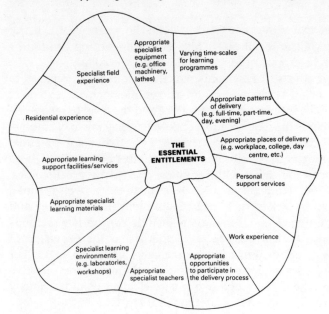

Figure 9.2 Common necessary elements
Source: FEU *Supporting Learning: Part 1 – A Model for Colleges* © FEU

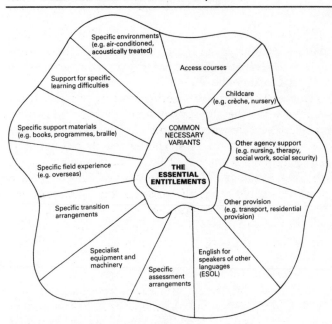

Figure 9.3 Specific necessary elements
Source: FEU *Supporting Learning: Part 1 – A Model for Colleges* © FEU

the more flexible the offer to all students. For example, the better the cross-college facilities, such as an open learning centre, the easier it is to support students in all parts of the college.

The core consists of elements which the college is prepared to provide for all students. It is a basic entitlement, the extent of which will be influenced by the nature and the level of resources. Core elements must be broadly conceived if they are to encourage increased participation. For example, information for potential students may need to be provided in a number of languages, or in other forms for those with language and literacy difficulties. Similarly, all students should be entitled to a well-planned curriculum. A lack of such a curriculum will affect teaching and learning. Other elements in the core include appropriate methods of assessment, clear performance criteria and the provision of technology and materials. In an inclusive approach to further education, core elements set basic requirements for effective provision. The absence of any one core element would seriously affect the quality of what is offered to students.

Common necessary variants are elements of provision necessary for an appropriate range of educational experiences. They may include such cross-college facilities as libraries and the provision of information technology or such facilities as laboratories, workshops and studios without which a broad range of curriculum options cannot be offered.

Common variants should also encompass appropriate patterns of and situations for the delivery of education programmes, varying time-scales for learning, specialist learning environments and support facilities and services. These variants are not concerned with individual needs. They reflect variations in environment, methodology, materials and experiences which are integral to a reasonable range of curricula and qualifications. Everybody taking science or computer studies will require a specialised environment. Anybody, on any course, might require personal or learning support, but the degree to which this is necessary will vary.

Specific necessary variants are required if participation is to be facilitated. Individuals may need particular forms of provision or support if they are to profit from the available educational opportunities. For example, child-care facilities or personal support for a physical disability may be required if a student is to follow a particular programme. This support need not be individual, it can often be pooled. It can take the form of a facility, for example a crèche, or the form of a service, such as a support team.

A well-managed college should meet these needs. They might include special environments, access courses, child-care assistance, specific assessment and examination arrangements, specially modified equipment and machinery, social work support and specific transition arrangements. In the model the examples given come from many aspects of college work. They envisage a parity of esteem for individuals, rather than a differential valuation of college work, and hence of students, on the basis of an academic hierarchy or fashion. They imply that meeting some needs of individuals with disabilities is not different in kind, for example, from meeting the requirements of very specialised high-level courses.

Management structure

The model leaves open the question of the college management structure; indeed, a pattern of core and variations can exist whatever the form of management. However, it is assumed that colleges will find it convenient to have a senior management team consisting of the principal, vice-principals and a director of administration.

Below this level the tradition has been to have departments, completely responsible for courses, of finite length, delivered to groups of students working in a particular field, such as engineering. Management structures are changing and many now have to take into account factors which include:

- development of subject and course modules, some of which may be common to a number of courses;
- accreditation of prior learning;
- development of individual programmes;
- development of cross-college open learning and learning support facilities.

(Modules may be subject elements such as mathematics, which are common, or they may be elements such as safety, hygiene, or, in the fullness of time, common elements in GNVQs.)

All these developments tend to break down traditional departmental boundaries. As a result, new management structures are being developed. Departments have been grouped in various ways to produce larger management units, still based on courses. Faculties have been formed based on the delivery of areas of the curriculum. As yet no common management structure has emerged, nor has the Further Education Staff College recommended one.

In most colleges separate empires still exist, cooperation between them is limited, responsibilities overlap and provision is duplicated. Colleges are seeking their own solutions, often on an *ad hoc* basis because of existing commitments to staffing and the expense of redundancy. Although all colleges are different, and differences are being encouraged in a further education market, there is a real need to develop effective structures for managing colleges in the future.

Using the model

The FEU publication *Supported Learning* also outlines a way in which the model might be used. A ten-stage process is suggested which summarises many of the aspects of management already discussed.

The audit and consultation   The first two stages involve a college audit and consultation with all the agencies already described.

Priorities   The next stage is seen as crucial. At this point governors, the principal and senior managers determine priorities and decide which college activities are to be included in the core and which are to be common, necessary and specific necessary variants. Decisions about the core, by implication, determine an entitlement for all students. These decisions must be taken in the light of the college's development plan, available resources and current demands.

Standards   The college sets standards, as targets, at the next stage. The provision of an element in the college programme is linked to the minimum and desired quality of its delivery. Quality criteria have to be determined on the basis of:

- whether staffing levels, staff qualifications and facilities are adequate for a particular form of provision;
- what changes might be necessary to achieve appropriate standards.

Resource management   Based on an effective audit of the college's resources and activities, carried out by senior management, governors, and if necessary, by external assessors, resource management takes place at this stage. The negotiation of training contracts will also be an occasion when resources are assessed in relation to defined training requirements. Questions asked at this stage include:

- What are the standards and costs of existing elements in the college programme?
- Are existing human and other resources adequate to deliver elements to the required standards??
- What reallocation of resources, or additional resources are necessary to raise the work to the desired standards?

Specialisms   The deployment of specialist knowledge and skills which cut across departmental and faculty structures needs to be considered next. Specialisms may include information technology, counselling and guidance, adult learning, the needs of students with disabilities and learning difficulties, gender and race and staff development.

Cross-curricular specialisms need to be identified and decisions taken about:

- how to deliver them;
- the roles and functions of co-ordinators for these specialisms;
- the role of senior managers in relation to these specialisms and their co-ordinators;
- how to develop general awareness of their contribution;
- how to provide other staff with a basic knowledge and skills in these specialisms.

Plans   This stage involves the development of a strategic, tactical and business plan based on decisions taken at earlier stages. Much will depend on the time-scale and requirements of funding mechanisms. Various concerns and public services have different planning cycles, and the college will need to be aware of them. Short-term and *ad hoc* funding will make it very difficult for colleges to carry through a strategic plan.

The strategic plan should set out the objectives for the long-term development of the college, the long-term shadow structure envisaged and being worked towards, and the standards it is aiming to achieve. The tactical plan should set out the short-term objectives and the next steps to be taken. Both plans will need to be linked with a business plan. They will need to be widely communicated and discussed and revised from time to time in the light of comment and events. Once decisions about the way forward have been reached, the next two stages are initiated.

Staff development   Most plans require the provision of staff development programmes (FEU 1987g; FEU 1989v) and staff appraisal schemes (Scribbins and Walton 1987) to implement them. Staff development should be part of a continuous process with three elements. These consist of the development of:

1) proficiency in general skills, such as the management of learning and curricular planning;
2) proficiency in specific areas of knowledge and of the skills related to different fields of work;
3) personal qualities and skills to enable individuals to make wider or different contributions.

Programme delivery   The penultimate stage is concerned with the delivery of the programmes that governors and senior management have agreed.

To do this, a number of questions have to be answered, including:

- What is to be delivered?
- To whom is it to be delivered?
- Where is it to be delivered?
- How is it to be delivered?
- What is the standard of delivery to be?
- What are the expected standards of the outcomes?

Evaluation   The final stage is concerned with evaluation, which is a continuing process. Although it represents a final stage, the form evaluation is going to take should be determined at the outset. How do you know what you have achieved unless you set objectives and decide how to evaluate them? Evaluation, which involves assessing standards, can only be effective when those carrying out the process are all clear about what they are assessing.

The performance indicators and criteria to be used for facilities, support services, teaching effectiveness, student performance and the outcomes of the work of staff and students must be defined. An evaluation must involve both quantitative and qualitative data. It must be based on clear criteria which can be understood not only by staff but also by students and their sponsors.

STAFF DEVELOPMENT

Creating change involves unsettling people, but effective change offers something more than discomfort. It should provide new interests and stimulation. Staff development is an essential part of a development plan. Although senior management will be able to provide much staff training from internal college resources by using the experience and expertise of existing staff it is also necessary to have external contributions to overcome inertia, to produce new ideas and to challenge existing practices.

Attempts are being made to establish quality standards for staff development. The FEU has completed field trials of Training and Lead Body Standards (TLDB) to establish their relevance to further education. This initiative (FEU Bulletin February 1992) sets out a framework for the qualification of staff in colleges which consists of modules at three levels. The field trials suggested that the scheme had some relevance but that modifications were necessary for the college setting.

This chapter has been primarily concerned with planning and introducing a more flexible approach to the management of colleges. There will be other models and other approaches but they will have in common many of the features outlined here, and Figure 9.4 sets out a framework for planning appropriate for them.

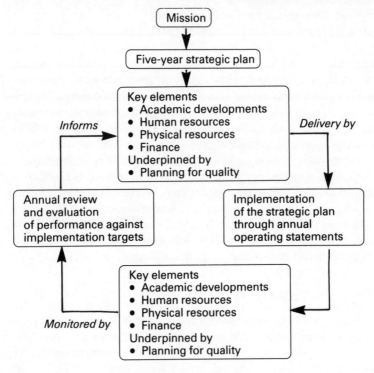

Figure 9.4 The FEFC Strategic Planning Framework
Source: FEFC

Chapter 10

A way ahead

While this book was being written great changes were taking place. The Education Reform Act (1988) was being implemented, and the Further and Higher Education Act (1992) passed and implemented. New methods of management and funding were being introduced. Now guidelines for future development have been laid down, but there remains much uncertainty about how post-sixteen provision will evolve.

The Further Education Funding Council (FEFC), established on 6 May 1992, has already consulted widely and been responsive to college concerns. A useful data-base is being established. Orders naming the colleges which became corporations under the Act were issued on 30 September 1991. On 1 April 1993 FEFC assumed responsibility for securing sufficient post-sixteen facilities, and colleges become corporations. After that date boards of corporation will be completely responsible for colleges but will no longer have members accountable to local electorates.

Responsibility for standards and quality will pass to the FEFC. The Office for Standards in Education (OFSTED) will no longer be concerned with standards in further education institutions. The FEFC will appoint its own inspectorate and HM Inspectorate will no longer work with colleges.

RESPONSIBILITIES AND ADMINISTRATION

Uncertainties remain as new legislation comes into force. New patterns of power and responsibility, for example, the relationship between the Department for Education (DFE) and the FEFC, will need to be worked out. The guidance issued by the Secretary of State and the annual level of funding for the Council will be very influential. Each college will need to establish relationships with the Council and its regional organisation. The Council's Regional Committees will have boundaries similar to those of the Department of Environment's regions.

THE CONTEXT

World trade agreements and the increasing commercial inter-dependence of nations will all have their effects on trade and industry and thus on further education and vocational preparation. European Community (EC) initiatives and guidelines for vocational training and professional qualifications will also be influential. Within this evolving situation the government's uncritical belief in market forces results in little planning and even less accountability to locally elected authorities.

A free market, in which the immediate needs of employers are met, is expected at the same time to identify long-term needs. Within a framework of short-term budgeting, colleges are expected to develop strategic plans to meet further education and training needs. Initiatives by individual colleges, together with output-related funding, are expected to provide equity in provision and opportunity.

During a period of continued economic uncertainty, it is only possible to identify a number of issues which colleges will need to consider as they are to develop a conceptual framework within which to make their contribution.

The international scene

The economic health of nations and their economic links with each other affect trade and industrial developments. New technologies and new patterns of trade influence the professional skills necessary for an efficient economy. While changes are difficult to predict, some trends are evident, for example, the increasing mobility of labour and the demand for a well-informed and qualified work-force.

What is now needed is a flexible approach to vocational qualifications, which allows for:

- skill modules to be combined in different forms;
- a work-force with proficiency in a second language;
- a system of world-class national qualifications which are compatible with those of other countries.

A number of factors have to be borne in mind, including:

- the likely effects of world economic developments on the pattern of industry, commerce and public services for which further education and vocational preparation are necessary;
- the effects of economic migration and refuge from strife and disaster;
- the extent to which regional trading arrangements will influence patterns of employment;
- the effect of EC guidelines for professional and technical qualifications, and their transferability, on college education and training programmes;
- the effects of the movement of students between EC countries on the work of colleges.

The development of a single market in the EC reinforces these trends. The Community has already outlined the patterns of vocational training it hopes to see developed and the ways in which open-distance learning systems might be developed (Comm (91) 397 & 398).

Studies in the EC have already indicated a pattern of student expectations and preferences. For example, students in the United Kingdom are far less willing to look for opportunities in other countries than their contemporaries in other EC countries. However, a number of further education colleges in the United Kingdom now have strong links with colleges in other countries. For some years they have provided UK qualifications for overseas students. More recently, colleges have been developing European links. Most colleges will have to forge links with post-sixteen provision in other EC countries and provide student programmes whose qualifications and outcomes are recognised in other countries.

The national scene

The national context for further and continuing education is far from settled. Institutions are now having to function in a context which divides responsibilities for post-sixteen education and training between the DFE, the Funding Agency for Schools, LEAs, the FEFC, the DE and TECs.

The Secretary of State for Education has delegated the following responsibilities to the FEFC:

- developing and consulting on a new funding methodology for subsequent years;
- establishing criteria for allocating capital funding determining the extent to which funds should be earmarked for specific purposes and how any such funds should be allocated;
- deciding on the criteria to be used in assessing applications to join the sector and proposals for the reorganisation of further education provision;
- making arrangements for ensuring that suitable provision is available for students with learning difficulties and disabilities;
- establishing a framework for discussing the quality of education in institutions in the sector, including the appointment of a quality assessment committee;
- offering guidance to its Regional Committees on the Council's requirements for advice.

Funding   This will be strictly controlled. The FEFC, although starting to fund on the basis of previous patterns of work, will be expected to develop strict cost-effective approaches to college provision.

Colleges are being encouraged to generate income, but the low level of economic activity in business and industry in the early 1990s will continue to make this difficult. The level of income from 'full-cost' courses may only become significant in a healthy economy.

Colleges are also expected to apply for sponsorship for making such provision in other institutions outside the college, in competition with other agencies. These new procedures systematise outreach work.

Competition   The relative independence of schools, further education colleges and other post-sixteen agencies may also lead to confusion in the short term as each institution competes for a limited market of students. A pattern, and perhaps a policy, is expected to emerge from such rivalry. Schools and colleges which prove most popular with parents, employers and students, and which produce the best results, are expected to survive and set standards.

The issues to be considered include:

- the effect of government economic policies and initiatives in trade and industry on patterns of employment;

- the extent of government influence on the FEFC and on colleges;
- responsibilities for identifying minority needs and ensuring that colleges meet them;
- responsibilities for ensuring an even distribution of post-sixteen opportunities;
- the means by which the financial contributions of different agencies can be coordinated to make effective use of available resources.

The college scene

Colleges play an important part in the transition of young people from school to work and of adults from unemployment to work. Transition programmes for most people, particularly school leavers, involve many other government and local authority departments and agencies. The college contribution should be an integral part of transition plans, but this requires close collaboration with other agencies.

Governors are now expected to undertake a wide range of responsibilities in a voluntary capacity. Colleges are faced with a number of demands, some of which may be conflicting. For example, they are expected to be entrepreneurial but also responsive to minority needs in their areas. They will be subjected to different political pressures, to favour talented and skilled applicants for places on the one hand, or to favour applicants who are disadvantaged and limited achievers on the other. Colleges need to be sure of their major responsibilities.

As they cope with or defend against change, the staff of colleges will have to recognise that they are entering into contractual relationships not only with sponsors of education and training but also with individual students. A statement of entitlements and expectations will become increasingly important.

Finally, the history of further education colleges has been one of striving for higher status: higher status within the college for higher-level work and higher status for colleges as they have progressed to advanced technology, polytechnic and university status. While this 'onward and upward' trend is of benefit to especially able students, it does little for the vocational standards of the main body of students on which industrial and commercial competition depends.

Among issues to be considered by colleges are:

- the influences, other than funding priorities, which bear on college priorities;
- the identification of, and provision for, community requirements for further education and vocational preparation;
- equitable provision for the whole range of further education needs in the population.

Colleges are now expected to develop strategic plans which will be subject to FEFC scrutiny. The outline for such plans is set out in Figure 9.4.

OTHER ISSUES

Priorities and unmet needs

Both the FEFC and TECs are expected to identify unmet further education and training needs, to take initiatives to ensure that provision is made for them and to determine how specific national training needs are to be met. There are inherent difficulties in a system where the boundaries of TECs are not the same as those of LEAs.

Policy limitations and student needs

Competition, efficiency and value for money, acceptable objectives of many policies, have one important limitation when resources are limited. Funding related to outcomes, and only available over limited time-spans, tends to give priority to the ablest and most easily trained students. The recruitment of these students is justified on the basis of their potential contribution to the economy.

There is a very real danger that the education and vocational preparation of some young people and adults will be given a low priority or neglected altogether. These potential students include individuals who may have been relatively unsuccessful in school, those who are not highly motivated, and those who may be hard to teach and train. If no attempt is made to meet their needs, new patterns of financing and responsibility may not raise the general level of competence of the work-force.

To raise the general level of the work-force is a national necessity, but the present system offers no incentive to accept challenging students. The lack of such inducements may lead to the same distribution of success and failure that was apparent in the old system. There should be rewards for taking on challenging students and turning young people and adults with poor attitudes and limited interests into successful trainees. The cost of not taking such initiatives has not yet been appreciated. It would be a pity if competition for able students perpetuated a system where the economic contribution of a well-trained elite was squandered on the social security support of a group whose further education is seen as unrewarding and of low priority.

Guidance and counselling

The post-sixteen free-for-all will be attractive to many but most people will require counselling and guidance in order to make an informed choice of education and training programme. Young people of school-leaving age may be especially vulnerable to pressures to stay on at school if they do not have an opportunity to discuss the range of post-sixteen possibilities with a disinterested adviser.

The role of the careers service may become increasingly important in post-sixteen guidance for young people as they choose appropriate courses of study. Parents, for example, may often encourage their children to stay on in school when in fact further education options may be better. They do not always understand the increasing complexity of the post-school phase. They too will often require the disinterested advice that an effective careers service can provide.

Alternative policies

At present there is a lack of alternative policy development. The government is fixed in its free-market approach. Opposition parties, while giving more priority to education, are often looking backwards to systems which were not particularly effective. The Further Education Staff College, which might be expected to be a centre of policy development, is in practice an agent for disseminating government policies. Its present role is under review.

There is an increasing need for an effective forum in which to develop alternative policies for further education and vocational training. It should be a forum where educational interests are well represented, where the relative merits of different forms of education and training are thrashed out with employers. It should be concerned with the education of the whole person and not narrowly confined to vocational proficiency.

Accountability

Until recently HM Inspectorate has had the responsibility of keeping the Secretary of State for Education informed about the standards of provision in colleges of further education. LEAs have had officers and advisors with responsibilities for further education provision. Governing bodies have also included elected members. In a number of ways colleges were accountable to local, independent and elected people.

The new legislation will ensure standards through funding mechanisms. Boards of college corporations will be self-appointed and no longer accountable to local electorates. They will be able to determine their own arrangements for quality control. Although the FEFC is appointing its own inspectorate, financial viability and profitability will be important external controls on the work of colleges.

EQUITY, OPPORTUNITY AND INDIVIDUALISED LEARNING

These three concepts sum up the philosophy of forward-looking further education. They need to be used as a test of how colleges respond in the further education market. Commercial pressures will make it more difficult to develop these three qualities.

Equity needs to be distinguished from equality. Equality of opportunity is not necessarily fair to all. It will be up to colleges, not funding bodies, to ensure that what they offer is accessible to the widest range of potential students and to ensure that all applications for education and training get a fair deal in an unfair world. All should be treated with equity.

Both the range of individual needs and the efficient use of resources demand the accreditation of prior learning and a modular approach to learning. Such an approach ensures that individuals can build up a programme which achieves the competences and qualifications they seek.

Opportunity is also related to access. Does the college provide a reasonable range of education and training opportunities to match the range of individual needs in the area served by the college? It may be easier to respond to the priorities of funding bodies than to drum up support for educational opportunities for minority groups. Because colleges are educational institutions they should be sensitive to all needs and not just to those that are easy to satisfy.

This book has looked at the present pattern of further education and training, at the changes taking place and at the implications of current policies for the future. The future cannot be predicted with any certainty. The aim has been to inform, clarify ideas and generate discussion.

When resources are limited authorities always stress the need for imagination and creativity. But the FEFC appears to mean what it says. It is consulting widely. It is making clear that the means by which further education and training are delivered is the concern of colleges. The FEFC will attempt to provide financial stability and support the most effective approaches to education and training developed by colleges. The Council is likely to reward initiative.

The combination of the efficient management of colleges, brought about by board members from industry and commerce, and educational imagination on the part of senior management, should lead to a period of effective provision by colleges. There are therefore many reasons for a modest optimism in spite of limited resources.

Colleges have always been more flexible than schools in their response to changing needs. They now have considerable freedom to respond independently and promptly to needs they identify and to the exciting challenges posed by a re-awakened interest in further education and training. The extent to which further education responds to these challenges will determine the skills and qualities which adults will contribute to commerce and industry in the United Kingdom, Europe and elsewhere.

Bibliography

ALBSU (1992) *Basic Skills in FE Colleges*.

Banks (1992) *The Essence of Total Quality Management*, Prentice Hall.

Birch, D. (1988) *Managing Resources in Further Education*, Bristol: FESC.

Business and Community Publications (227a City Road, London EC1V 1LX):
  A Vision for TECs.
  TECs Partnership with Education.
  TECs and Disability – Action Issues.
  TECs Customised Training and Targetted Recruitment.

CBI (1989) *Towards a Skills Revolution* London: CBI.

DE (1990) *Training Credits for Young People*.

DE/NIACE/REPLAN (1989) *Opportunities for the Older Unemployed*.

DES (1987) *Managing Colleges Efficiently*, London: HMSO.

DES (1991) White Paper *Education and Training for the 21st Century*, London: HMSO.

Education Reform Act (1988), London: HMSO.

Edwards, J. (1991) *Evaluation in Adult and Further Education*, London: WEA.

EOC/FEU (1989–90) *Gender Newsletters*.

FEFC (1992) Circulars 92.14, 92/17, 92/17.

FESC (1986) *Managing Space in Colleges*.

FESC (1991) *Managing the College Budget*.

FESC (1991a) *Individual Development Plans*.

FESC (1991b) *What is a College?*

FESC (1991c) *Managing and Governing Staff*.

FESC (1991d) *Marketing Colleges*.

FESC (1991e) *College Organisation and Structures*.

FESC (1991f) *Governors and Resource Management*.

FESC (1991g) *Strategic Planning and Management*.

FESC (1991h) *Governors and the Curriculum*.

FESC (1991i) *College Properties and Premises*.

FEU/DTI (1989) *Promoting Enterprise*.

FEU/FESC (1985) *Marketing Further and Higher Education*.

FEU/FESC (1988) *Managing Resources in FE*.

FEU/NIACE (1992) *Quality Education and Training for the Adult Unemployed*.

FEU/REPLAN (1988a) *A Second Chance to Learn.*
FEU/REPLAN (1988b) *Out reach and Inreach.*
FEU/REPLAN (1989a) *Working with Young Adults in a Multicultural Context.*
FEU/REPLAN (1989b) *Developing Education and Training for the Adult Unemployed.*
FEU/REPLAN (1989c) *Opportunities for the Older Unemployed.*
FEU/REPLAN (1989d) *Negotiating the Curricula of Unemployed Adults.*
FEU/REPLAN (1989e) *The Outreach College.*
FEU/REPLAN (1990) *Providing for Adults.*
FEU (1986–9) Bulletins 1–11 *Developing Planning in NAFE.*
FEU (1987a) *Who Needs IT?*
FEU (1987b) *Information Technology Support Systems for Education and Training.*
FEU (1987c) *Access to Further and Higher Education.*
FEU (1987d) *Quality in NAFE.*
FEU (1987e) *Implementing Open Learning in LEA Institutions.*
FEU (1987f) *Relevance, Flexibility and Competence.*
FEU (1987g) *Planning Staff Development: A Guide for Managers.*
FEU (1988a) *Reaching out to Rural Learners.*
FEU (1988b) *Adult Education and Training in a Rural Area.*
FEU (1988c) *Staff Development for a Multicultural Society.*
FEU (1988d) *Equal Opportunities for Ethnic Minorities.*
FEU (1988e) *Establishing a Personal Guidance Base in Two Colleges.*
FEU (1988f) *The Role of Guidance in Education and Training.*
FEU (1988g) *Learning by Doing.*
FEU (1988h) *Planning the FE Curriculum. Implications of the 1988 Education Reform Act.*
FEU (1988i) *Coping with Crisis.*
FEU (1988j) *Training for Curriculum Development.*
FEU (1988k) *The Evaluation of Open Learning Materials.*
FEU (1988l) *Access to the Mainstream Curriculum.*
FEU (1989a) *The Youth Work Curriculum.*
FEU (1989b) *Language in Education.*
FEU (1989c) *The Concept of Key Technologies.*
FEU (1989d) *Extending Links in New Technology Training.*
FEU (1989e) *National Vocational Qualifications.*
FEU (1989f) *Mainstream Curricula in a Multicultural Society.*
FEU (1989g) *National Vocational Qualifications. Broadsheets 1–6.*
FEU (1989h) *The Implications of Competence Based Curricula.*
FEU (1989i) *Equal Opportunities: Policy and Practice.*
FEU (1989j) *Learning to Manage.*
FEU (1989k) *Towards an Educational Audit.*
FEU (1989l) *Making a Curricula Response.*
FEU (1989m) *Implications of a Competence Based Curriculum.*
FEU (1989n) *Supporting the Unemployed in Further Education.*
FEU (1989o) *Skills Assessment and Vocational Guidance for the Unemployed.*
FEU (1989p) *Local Innovation in Adult Education and Training.*
FEU (1989q) *Modularisation in Adult Education and Training.*
FEU (1989r) *Towards a Framework for Curriculum Entitlement.*

FEU (1989s) *Flexible Learning in Perspective*.

FEU (1989t) *Learning Support*.

FEU (1989u) *The Strategic Planning of Further Education*.

FEU (1989v) *Training for Curriculum Development*.

FEU (1990a) *Development Programmes for Further Education Governors*.

FEU (1990b) *Individuality in Learning*.

FEU (1990c) *Access Funds for Further Education. A Planning Checklist*.

FEU (1990d) *Planning Further Education. Equal Opportunities for People with Disabilities or Special Educational Needs*.

FEU (1990e) *Planning Human Resource Development through Equal Opportunities*.

FEU (1990f) *Developing a Marketing Strategy for Adult and Continuing Education*.

FEU (1990g) *Implementing Pick-Up in LEA Colleges*.

FEU/PICK-UP (1990h) *Training for Small and Medium Companies*.

FEU/PICK-UP (1990i) *Training for Full-time Officers of Trade Unions*.

FEU (1990j) *Individuality in Learning*.

FEU (1990k) *Training for the Future*.

FEU (1991a) *Working with Europe*.

FEU (1991b) *Access to IT Organisation. development strategies for providers of training for women*.

FEU (1991c) *Quality Matters*.

FEU (1991d) *Flexible Colleges* (Parts 1 and 2).

FEU (1991e) *FE Colleges and Innercity Regeneration: A Strategy for Action*.

FEU (1992a) *Colleges Going Green*.

FEU (1992b) *The Assessment of Prior Learning and Learner Services*.

FEU (1992c) *A Basis for Credit*.

FEU (1992d) *Getting to Grips with Education and Training for Industry*.

FEU (1992e) *Supporting Learning: Part 1 – A Model for Colleges* .

FEU (1992f) *The Assessment of Workbased Learning*.

FEU (1992g) *Core Skills in Action*.

FEU (1992h) *Training and Development Lead Body Standards in Further Education*.

FEU (1992i) *A New Life*.

FEU (1992j) *Resourcing Tomorrows College*.

FEU/UDACE (1992) *Understanding Accreditation*.

Hall (1990) *Maintained Further Education in the United Kingdom*, Bristol: FESC.

Industry Matters (1988) *New Governors for Further Education*.

Kedney, McAllister and Varley (1990) *Implementing ERA in Colleges*, Bristol: FESC.

Lyton Gray, ed. (1991) *Managing Colleges in a Changing World*, Bristol: FESC.

McNay, I., ed. (1991) *Post-Compulsory Education*, Milton Keynes: Open University Press.

OECD (1990) *Labour Market Policies for the 1990s*, Paris: OECD.

Richardson, B.R. (1989) *Business Planning: An Approach to Strategic Management*, London: Pitman.

Scribbins, K. and Walton, F. (1987) *Staff Appraisal in Further Education and Higher Education*, Bristol: FESC.

Theodossin, E. (1989a) *The Responsive College*, Bristol: FESC.
—— (1989b) *Marketing the College*, Bristol: FESC.
TEED (1990) *The Management of Quality BS 5750 and Beyond*, London: HMSO.
White Paper (1990) *Our Common Inheritance*, London: HMSO.

Index

ability range 39
access 34, 96, 121; to college 54–5
access courses 44, 45, 55
access funds 43
accommodation 97, 98–9
accountability 120
accreditation 87–8; of prior learning 35, 86, 97, 120–1
active retirement group 35
administrative services *see* management
admission procedures 55–6, 100–1
adult education 22–3, 62, 63
adult literacy 54
Adult Literacy and Basic Studies Unit (ALBSU) 22, 63
adult students 34–5, 42–5
age range of students 33, 34, 39
Appendix II provision 20
assessment 68; *see also* standards
assessor's perspective 84, 95
attainment, range of 39
audit, educational 102–3, 109

backgrounds, students' 40
budgeting 52
buildings 97, 99
business plan 96, 103, 109
Business Technician Education Certificate (BTEC) 21

careers guidance 40, 45, 55, 65, 69, 119; *see also* support services
change, climate of 7

child care 34, 45
City and Guilds of London Institute 17, 60
city technical colleges 17
collaboration 98–9
colleges: and competition 5–6, 36, 44, 116; dynamic organisations 81; flexible 92–4; funding 5, 15, 26, 50, 62, 118; and the future 117– 8; industrial development and 16–17; links with schools 21–2, 55; procedural changes 50–6; responsiveness to change 49, 61; and sponsors 45–6; and status 17, 118; structural change 62–71; and training agencies 9–11, 23–4, 25; transition to learner-centredness 92–4; values 12; vital centres in community 14–15; young people's perception of 33
commercial influences on further education 10, 30–1
common necessary elements 104, 105, 106–7
community (local) 14–15
competences 8–9, 35, 83–4
competition 36, 98; for funds 51; for students 5–6, 53, 75, 116–7
Confederation of British Industry (CBI) 7, 9, 31
cost-effectiveness 96–7
consultation: by colleges 104, 110; by government 36–7

core provision 104, 105, 106
counselling 55, 65, 67, 69, 82–3,
    119; *see also* support services
cross-college provision 64–5,
    67–70, 97
curriculum 100; models of 57–8
curriculum development 56, 59,
    66–7

degree courses 17
demographic change 32–5
Department of Education and
    Science (DES) 18–19, 26, 65;
    1991 White Paper 15, 26–7
Department of Employment (DE)
    44, 51, 65–6, 75, 115; and FEFC
    113–14
Department of Further Education
    (DFE) (previously DEF) 75, 97,
    115
departments, college 62, 109
differentiated learning 86–7
disabilities, students with 42, 59,
    104
disenchanted learners 14, 38, 41–2;
    outreach work 54, 77, 82; policy
    limitations and 118–19

education: industrial development
    and 16–17; and training 7–9; *see
    also* adult education, further
    (and continuing) education
Education Act (1944) 17–18
Education Reform Act (1988) 24,
    32, 113; and LEAs 9–10, 25, 42,
    51
employers 31; collaboration with
    50, 53–4; funding training 43, 75
Employment Act (1988) 24
employment training (ET) 25,
    41–2, 46
Employment Training Grants 43
enterprise culture 36–7; *see also*
    competition
entitlement 6, 70–1; and standards
    84–5
environmental concern 28–9
equal opportunities 31, 44–5, 78,
    90; *see also* values

equity 11–15, 47, 96, 120–1; *see
    also* inclusiveness
ethnic groups 34–5, 41, 44
European Community (EC) 29, 88,
    114, 115
evaluation (of planning) 111
evening classes 16–17

flexible learning 92–4
Francis, H. 56–7
funding: for colleges 5, 15, 26, 50,
    62, 118; for further
    education/training 31, 43, 44,
    65–6, 75, 89–90; priorities 88–9
Funding Agency for Schools 115
further (and continuing) education:
    aims and objectives 6–7, 77–8,
    81; definitions in Schedule 2
    76–7; influences on 28–37, 89–
    90, 114–7; new recognition of
    value 15; recent history 16–27;
    traditional view of 5;
    undervalued 3–4; youth service,
    adult education and 22–3
Further Education Funding Council
    (FEFC) 5, 27, 62, 75, 115, 121;
    capital works 97; college
    submissions to 79, 89; colleges'
    planning 101, 103, 112;
    inspection 19, 121; mergers 99;
    minority needs 37; priorities 10,
    15, 88, 89–90; quality assurance
    84; responsibilities 113–14,
    116–18; students with
    disabilities and learning
    difficulties 42; training credits
    76; Vesting Date 113
Further Education Staff College
    (FESC) 19, 108; curriculum
    development 59; lack of
    alternative policy development
    119–20; staff development 60
Further Education Unit (FEU);
    curriculum development 59, 66;
    flexible colleges 92–4; influence
    on further education 19–20; in-
    service education 60; planning
    model 102, 103–11; quality
    94–5; *Training for the Future*

96; Training and Lead Body Standards 111
Further and Higher Education Act (1992) 15, 17, 23, 25, 27, 113; Schedule 2, 63, 76–7

General National Vocational Qualifications (GNVQ) 32, 35, 56, 66, 84
global influences 28–9
government policies 23–7, 30, 31, 89; adult education 63; aims of legislation 75–6; competition 5–6, 76; constant change 7; consultation 36–7; enterprise culture 36; funding 24–5, 26; lack of alternatives to 19, 20; limitations and student needs 118–19; new recognition of further education 15; standards 76, 94
governors 25, 52, 117
guidance, personal 55, 69, 82–3, 119; see also careers guidance, support services

Her Majesty's Inspectorate (HMI) 18–19, 50, 113, 120
home working 43–4

inclusiveness 20–1, 47–8, 52, 104; and student potential 79–80; see also equity
independence and values 9–11, 78–9
individualised learning 120–1
industrial development 16–17
industrial influences on further education 30–1, 32
information technology 43–4; see also new technologies
Inner London Education Authority (ILEA) 20
in-service education 60
integration, philosophy of 42
interactive learning 86
international influences on further education 28, 29–30, 114–15

labour market 29, 30–1

learner-centred colleges 92–4
learner-led curriculum model 57, 58, 59
learning: conditions for 85–7; cross-college provision of facilities for 67, 68–9, 97; differentiated 86–7, 98; flexible 92–4; individualised 120–1; interactive 86, 98; prior see prior learning; range of rates/styles 39; support services 69, 80, 83
learning difficulties, students with 42, 59, 104
learning strategies 56–9
local education authorities (LEAs) 115; accountability 120; Discretionary Awards 43; Education Reform Act 9–10, 25, 42, 51; further education sections 50; maintenance of buildings 97; and planning 50–1, 89; post-war development of further education 18–19; role in funding 62, 65, 75, 88, 89; students with disabilities and learning difficulties 42

maintenance of buildings 97, 99
management 49, 62, 96, 98–9; FEU planning model 107–8; structural change 68, 69–70, 90
Manpower Services Commission (MSC) 23–4; see also Training Agency
marketing 53–4, 81–2, 99; niche 36
Mechanics' Institutes 16–17
minority groups 12–14, 37
modular courses 64, 66–7, 108, 120–1

national context for further education 116–18
national curriculum 32
National Extension College 87
national influences on further education 30–2
National Vocational Qualifications (NVQs) 31, 35, 56, 64, 84; accreditation schemes 66–7,

87–8; *see also* General National
Vocational Qualifications
needs: minority groups 12–14, 37;
policy limitations and
challenging students 118–19;
range of students' 40; unmet 118
needs analysis 81–2
networks 98
new technologies 4, 23, 30, 32, 43–4
New Training Initiative 24
niche marketing 36
Non-Advanced Further Education
Steering Group 24
non-teaching staff 60

Office for Standards in Education
(OFSTED) 113
Open College 63
open learning 87
open learning centres 68
opportunity 121–2; *see also* equal
opportunities
organisation 49, 62, 99–100; new
patterns 64–71
outreach work 16, 54
overseas students 54

packages, course 53–4
participation, increased 81–3
Pick-Up Programme 54–5
performance indicators 95; *see also*
quality standards
planning 50–2, 102–12; FEFC
guidance 101, 103, 112; FEU
model 103–11; staff
development 110, 111–112
plant (buildings) 97, 98–99
policy *see* government policy
prior learning: accreditation 35, 86,
97, 120–1; assessing 56, 80;
variety of 40
procedures: changes in 50–6;
cross-college 67, 68
programme delivery 111
providers 79
purchasers 79

qualifications, vocational 16, 17,
35; awarding bodies 18;

internationally acceptable
115–16; *see also* General
National Vocational
Qualifications, National
Vocational Qualifications
quality 83–5, 94–6
quality assurance 54, 84, 95, 96
quality control 95

recurrent education 45
Regional Further Education
Advisory Councils 18, 50
regional influences on further
education 32
resource management 52, 96–7, 109
retraining 44
Royal Society of Arts 17, 60

school-leavers 20, 41
schools: colleges' competition with
5–6, 53, 75, 116; disenchanted
learners 14; inequalities 11;
links with colleges 21–2, 55
Scotland 66
skills 35; competences and 7–9;
core 59; multi-skill development
43
specialisms 109–10
specific necessary variants 105,
107, 108
sponsorship: college 89; of students
45–6
staff appraisal 95, 110
staff development 59–60, 110,
111–112
staffing 59–60
standards: entitlement and 84–5;
improving 83–5, 94–6
structural change 62–71
students 79, 82; with disabilities
and learning difficulties 42, 59,
105; disenchanted *see*
disenchanted learners;
expectations/preferences 29,
116; inclusiveness and potential
of 79–80; population 32–5,
38–48; sponsorship 45–6
support services 40, 45, 47, 55, 65,
100; cross-college provision 67,

69; *see also* careers guidance, counselling

tactical plans 103, 110
teacher education 59–60
teaching strategies 56–9
technical schools 17
Technical Vocational Education Initiative (TVEI) 21–2, 25, 46, 65; Steering Group 24
technology, new 4, 23, 30, 32, 43–4
training 4; education and 7–9; retraining 44; *see also* employment training, youth training
training agencies 9–11, 12; *see also under individual names*
Training Agency 12, 49, 51, 65, 66, 70; and further education 21, 23–4
Training Credits 75–6, 88–9, 97
Training, Education and Enterprise Directorate (TEED) 24, 25
Training and Enterprise Councils (TECs) 24–5, 49, 89, 99, 116; conflicting priorities/procedures 25, 119; employers and 31; and FEFC 76; funding role 5, 62, 65–6, 75; priorities 46, 88; students with disabilities 13; unmet needs 118
Training and Lead Body Standards (TLDB) 111–12
Training and Occupation Classification (TOC) 26

transition programmes 117
tutoring 55, 69; *see also* support services
twilight classes 16

unemployment 44; youth 21, 23, 38
Unit for the Development of Adult Continuing Education (UDACE) 19–20
unmet needs 118

values 90; equity and 11–15; independence and 9–11, 78–9; variations in students' 40
vocational education, defining 76–7
vocational qualifications *see* General National Vocational Qualifications, National Vocational Qualifications, qualifications

Warnock Report 42
women: entering further education 34; entering the labour market 44–5
work-related non-advanced further education (WRNAFE) 24, 25, 46

young people 33–4, 40–2
youth service 22–3, 63–4, 77
youth training (YT) 25, 34, 41–2, 46
Youth Training Board 24
youth unemployment 21, 23, 38; *see also* unemployment